T0109402

ADVANCED SURVIVAL

ADVANCED SURVIVAL

A GUIDE TO THE SELF-RELIANCE REVOLUTION

James C. Jones

Skyhorse Publishing

Skyhorse Publishing books may be purchased in bulk at special discounts for sales promotion, corporate gifts, fund-raising, or educational purposes. Special editions can also be created to specifications. For details, contact the Special Sales Department, Skyhorse Publishing, 307 West 36th Street, 11th Floor, New York, NY 10018 or info@skyhorsepublishing.com.

Skyhorse® and Skyhorse Publishing® are registered trademarks of Skyhorse Publishing, Inc.®, a Delaware corporation.

Visit our website at www.skyhorsepublishing.com.

10 9 8 7 6 5 4 3 2 1

Library of Congress Cataloging-in-Publication Data is available on file.

Cover design by Tom Lau
Cover photo credit: iStockphoto

Print ISBN: 978-1-5107-3899-7
Ebook ISBN: 978-1-5107-3901-7

Printed in the United States of America.

CONTENTS

PREFACE

All the chapters except for "Storm Warning" and "Energy" were written exclusively for this book, but some of them have since been used in their original or modified forms in Live Free's *American Survivor* newsletter. The subjects covered are intended as a starting point and guide rather than a complete manual. Many of these subjects—including water, food, home defense, and medical care—are well addressed in many volumes available to the reader. I tried to include some practical how-to information with each chapter, but the reader is advised to pursue further study and practical trial-and-error learning. Many of these skills can be pursued as hobbies or with groups that build support networks as well as sharing skills. I included "Storm Warning" as an imperative for the actions recommended in the chapters that follow and "Food, Famine, and Power" and "Energy" because they put the relationship between these key factors for sustainable population and economic stability in perspective.

INTRODUCTION AND PERSPECTIVE

Iwas born at the end of the steam age and at the beginning of World War II. My father was a stationary engineer, so I have memories of the odors of burning coal, hot metal, and steam. I was comfortable in engine rooms among the hiss and chug of pistons and the whine of flywheels. My early memories also include blackouts, block wardens, duck-and-cover drills, and weekly reports of nuclear tests. I grew up with gasoline-gulping automobiles and massive consumerism and waste. Everyone thought that we would have more and more and go further and further without consequences or cost. At one time I dreamed of being an astronaut. The hope was that we could colonize the moon and planets using solar power, hydroponics, and other technologies to survive and build on hostile planets. Now, as we run out of cheap fuels and our economies decline, we turn to these technologies to survive on this planet as *it* becomes more hostile.

The massive use of America's resources and labor created a reserve of wealth that I saw in my youth. Unfortunately, greed, wastefulness, and apathy over the past decades used up those resources and financial wealth, and have run on debt, denial, and false hope for the past forty years. In the past centuries when people used up a land or ruined a society, they just moved on, but the "new world" is done and there is no place to go. We cannot run or hide from our situation.

The grim reality is that we cannot sustain this population at this level of civilization much longer. The idea that we can bring the whole planet to the living standard of America with two, three, or four times the population is absurd. Significant population reductions are inevitable through famine, epidemics, conflicts, and attrition. Shortages of critical materials and the effects of climate change on food production, water availability, and destruction of communities will reach crisis proportions. Ultimately a balance will be restored where a smaller population lives well and continues to push toward a better future. Who those survivors are and what they do with the future is the vital question of this millennium. It is a question to be answered by the readers of this book and their children. After a century of dependent living and regulated life, it will be challenging to adapt and restore independence and freedom through self-reliance.

This book can only provide an outline and some basic methodologies for addressing the various life needs and challenges of this revolutionary transformation. If good people prepare to survive and then act to become self-reliant, American values and ideals will prevail as the foundation for the future.

1

Storm Warning

- In the twentieth century, we put in less and less and took more and more.
- In the twenty-first century, survivors will be the ones who do more and more with less and less.
- The twentieth century was the time of waste and consumption and luxury.
- The twenty-first century will be the time of conservation and self-reliance.

THE PERFECT STORM OF CHANGE AND DISASTER IN THE YEARS TO COME AND HOW TO PREPARE FOR IT

In the movie *The Matrix,* Agent Smith (a virtual being) observes, "Humans are the only mammal that acts more like a parasite, moving from one area to the next while growing exponentially until all of the resources in one area are gone and the area is dead and then moving on to the next area." In fact, archeological and anthropological data support this assertion. The arrival of humans always correlates to extinctions of animal, vegetable, and mineral resources. In cases such as islands where the human population was unable to move on, they fought with each other over the few remaining resources and then died out or lingered in misery and poverty.

In the twentieth century, America populated and consumed itself into a dead end. America was the last place to go, and now there is no place to move on to. The entire world is now populated beyond the remaining resources. We have a fast-growing population seeking higher living standards on a nearly used-up planet. There are as many people alive now as there were during the whole of recorded history combined, and that will double in the next forty years. Windmills, hydrogen power, solar power, and better farming will buy a little time, but this is a race that humanity cannot win. The use of corn for fuel has instantly caused a food shortage. Many stores in the United States have already experienced shortages of rice and other staples. Africa is starving and there have been food riots in Egypt, the Philippines, and Mexico. As of 2018, fifty-one countries have declared being in a food crisis. Some countries have banned exports of grain to ensure local supplies.

The falling value of the dollar has resulted in more of them being needed to buy the same amount of oil. The drive for biofuel is leading to fewer food crops and massive deforestation in third world countries. Grain reserves are at a thirty-year low. A bad harvest anywhere could be catastrophic. Massive legal and illegal immigration from "have not" to "still have" nations is generating instability, crime, and unrest throughout Europe and the United States, and this will only get worse. In some cases food is the new drugs. Criminal gangs known as "boosters" are beginning to steal food and resell it on the streets. The "black market" and government price controls will be more and more evident over the next five to ten years.

Water is the new oil. There are already legal conflicts developing between states in the United States and between many foreign nations over access to water. Water is currently classified as a "resource" belonging to everyone, but that could change. There are motions afoot to classify water as a "commodity" to be owned, bought, and sold like oil. Think about the consequences of that! Even freedom from thirst may not be a human right. Urban sprawl is eating up farmland. When I was a boy, I lived on the edge of Chicago at 97th Street South. There were open marshes, woods, and farms nearby. Now, sixty years later, I have to go out to 225th Street to see similar areas, and that is being developed quickly. With exponential growth, Chicago's sprawl could reach the Mississippi by the end of the century.

The oceans are no longer international territory. As resources dwindle, nations are reaching out for the ocean and the ocean floors. The Russians recently planted their flag on the sea floor at the North Pole to claim any mineral resources that may be there. Other nations are trying to extend their boundaries or are disputing current limits. There is no doubt that in the future, every inch of the Earth's land, ice, and water area will be claimed by someone. This will of course result in serious border conflicts and probably wars.

Americans once lived the "American dream" with one working parent, good vacations, and benefits, while buying with cash and saving regularly. Today it takes two working parents taking few vacations with few benefits and high debt to desperately hang on to a vanishing dream. As the late comedian George Carlin said, "We spent money we didn't have on stuff we didn't need"—and now we are broke with a lot of junk. The politicians will continue to try to fool the public with smoke and mirrors to get reelected, and since false hope gets more votes than hard choices, the issues will not be faced. So there will be an ever-increasing series of ups and downs, but the downs will always be greater than the ups. The elite will thrive, the unprepared will perish, and the prepared will survive and stay free.

WHAT WILL HAPPEN?

In essence, the entire social, economic, political, and environmental structure of the planet will be progressively stressed to the breaking point. Virtually everything we consider "normal" will be subject to change.

Cuts in police, fire, and medical services will put every family in growing danger. Trauma centers in cities and suburbs are already closing at an alarming rate.

The aging infrastructure will continue to degenerate faster than it can be maintained, causing failures in power distribution, water service, sewer systems, bridges, and roadways.

Natural disaster will become more and more lethal due to the increased population densities, a more dependent population, and declining emergency services.

Climate changes will kill hundreds of thousands. Climatologists agree that heat waves lasting weeks with temperatures of 110°–120°F will be common in cities like Chicago and New York by the end of the century. Don't even think about Arizona or California! Recent heat waves in Chicago and France killed thousands. As the population doubles and the sources of water and energy for air conditioning diminish, heat alone could be enough to bring down civilization. The fire season in California used to be a few months in the 1990s but is all year now. There is a clear water path through the North Polar cap.

No doubt, epidemics and pandemics will occur, with or without terrorist involvement. It is simply a natural phenomenon when populations become too dense. There are millions of viruses that could mutate and spread more quickly than they can be controlled. Bubonic plague hit India as recently as 1994. Influenza killed millions in the last century and mutates constantly. Antibiotics are becoming less and less effective, and resistant viruses are multiplying every year. Experts agree that a worldwide pandemic is likely within the next ten to twenty years.

The power of gangs and international criminal organizations will grow dramatically as they begin to control access to food, medications, and other vital needs. The so-called "black market" will return. The gangs will often be able to offer better protection than the state. This is already a fact in poorer communities and third world countries. Citizens may have a choice between being a ward and slave of a corrupt and oppressive state or a member of a brutal gang.

Prices will continue to rise faster than income. Paper money will become increasingly worthless. This will dump the lower-income people and smaller businesses into bankruptcy. Service workers (such as landscapers, waiters, cleaners, and general labor) will be the first to go, followed by semiskilled workers. Being poor is a bad survival plan.

Shortages of just about everything will result in rationing, price gouging, increased theft, violence, and the rise of the "black market," as in "I know a guy that can score you some cornmeal."

Massive legal and illegal immigration will occur as people flee from countries where the economies, food supplies, and water sources are already inadequate. These refugees will flee to any adjoining country where prospects are even a little better. This trend will result in increased border conflicts and civil disorder.

State and national governments will greatly increase regulations and confiscation (laws and taxes) in an attempt to sustain programs and authority. They may well attempt to institute socialist economics and unconstitutional laws. Hungry and desperate people will accept false promises of security in exchange for their (and your) freedoms. Even the Constitution and Bill of Rights will be at risk of being scrapped.

When things get tough, those who seem to be doing okay will be regarded with suspicion and even anger. We are talking about the folks who stayed out of debt and were better prepared to survive. The politicians will gladly blame them for hoarding, conspiring, and hurting the economy. They will do this to deflect blame from themselves and their associates.

Demigods and fanatics of all kinds will rise out of the chaos to offer solutions that will involve hate, violence, obedience, and the surrender of freedoms and property. They will be more dangerous to survival than any of the manmade or natural disasters that may have occurred.

Local governments are closer to the people and will struggle to cope with changing conditions. Some may collapse, some may become corrupt, but some may restructure to involve citizen volunteers, local food co-ops, and other innovations to maintain and secure their communities.

This will all work out in one of three ways:

1. There will be one or more population-reducing events such as wars, pandemics, famines, or other disasters that will bring the population to a sustainable level where "life, liberty, and the pursuit of happiness" can still exist.
2. The entire society will degenerate into a constant state of conflict on a local and world basis. In this scenario, the wealthy elite and the gang leaders will live well, while the masses obey, pay, and struggle to survive.
3. The world population will exist in a regulated, pacified, crowded, and meaningless subsistence existence under the rule of a world state.

Exactly what will happen, how it will happen, and how soon it will happen are hard to predict, but grim and dangerous changes will happen. There will be three groups of people involved in these struggles.

- Predators exist on the bottom and top of society. They believe they have the right to take the property, freedom, and even the lives of others. On the top end, we have the politicians, bureaucrats, ultra-rich, and corporate executives. Of course, they are not all evil conspirators (some may be), but as a culture they tax, price, exploit, manipulate, regulate, and confiscate. On the bottom, we have the "criminal class" that steals, intimidates, drugs, destroys, and murders. When things get tough, these people thrive and multiply like rats. The rules and natural inhibitions that kept them in check tend to break down. They will steadily fight over the decreasing resources of the general population. They have always survived at the expense of the welfare and safety of good and hard-working people. But in the hard times to come they will survive at the expense of the very survival of those people.

- Victims are the great majority of the world population that remains in denial of reality and dependent on others for survival. In the poorer communities and countries, it is people who even now are barely able to obtain enough food, water, and shelter to get by from day to day. They exist in dwindling resources and the excess of the wealthier. These resources and excesses will continue to diminish with predictable and horrible results. In the richer nations it is the middle class that works harder and harder for less and less in the face of increasing debt, crime, and taxation. They have more time but are on the same road to losing life, liberty, and property.

- Survivors are people who are not dependent on exploiting others or being supported by others. They take full responsibility for the sustenance and security of themselves and their families. While they are hardworking and productive members of society, they have not become fully dependent on that society. While they enjoy life, they avoid waste, unnecessary consumption, and debt. They tend to live a bit below their means and have at least some reserves and backup systems if things get bad. Their sense of responsibility makes them good citizens and good neighbors who are often involved in volunteer work. In the gravest extremes, most of them will manage to stay alive without harming others or surrendering basic freedoms.

Predators will say, "Let me save you." Victims will say, "Who will save me?" Survivors will say, "Let's save ourselves together."

WHAT CAN WE DO?

To quote yet another movie, *Terminator 3: Rise of the Machines,* "We were not intended to prevent the catastrophe, just to survive it." You must survive without becoming predators or victims or slaves. You and your family have the mission of surviving physically, mentally, morally, and spiritually. Compassion, knowledge, responsibility, freedom, and hope must survive with you. The past belongs to those who took more and more while giving back less and less. The future belongs to those who can do more with less and fight those who would take what is not theirs. The past was the age of dependency and waste. The future must be the age of self-reliance and efficiency. You and your family must be ready and able to adapt to painful and deadly changes. You must be ready to outlast, outsmart, and even outfight the predators and opportunists who will victimize the unprepared. While it may or may not be necessary to "take to the hills" or drop off the grid entirely, you must consider that possibility. Meanwhile, you need to change your habits and take serious steps to improve your survivability before it's too late.

- Reduce your "needs" and consumption. There is a big difference between what society calls "needs" and what you really need. Society says you need golf, brand-name coffee, designer clothes, every new DVD that comes out, and bottled water. Most tap water exceeds bottled water in safety, beats bottled water in blind taste tests, and is 240 to 10,000 times cheaper. Stop using credit cards to buy everyday items. Cash makes you think and see what you are spending. Resist fast foods. Brown-bagging or home cooking is much cheaper and healthier. You do not need to go to a health club to get exercise. Walking, home exercise, gardening, and other activities along with a good diet will do the job, but you do need to have will power. Leave the coffee, health club, designer labels, fast food, and credit card rip-offs to the future victims.

And, of course, you don't need to smoke. That eats up your money and endangers your life.

- Change your investments. Move at least 50 percent of your wealth out of paper assets—such as stocks and money market accounts—and into such tangible assets as real estate, precious metals, tools, trade goods, and life-critical supplies.

- Spend frugally. I am not advocating an Amish lifestyle. Treat yourself occasionally, go out to dinner from time to time, but stop wasting your financial resources. They are not endless, and what you waste today you cannot get back for what you may really need later.

- Stop wasting resources. Use real plates and cups instead of paper plates and cups for everyday meals. Use washable rags instead of paper towels. Use all the contents of containers of food and household cleaners. Turn off lights in rooms that are empty. Plan "right-sized" meals that leave a clean plate without an overfull stomach. This will save money while you lose a little of that extra weight. Here's a good weight loss tip: you do not need to eat every time you feel hungry! Rain barrels on downspouts can catch thousands of gallons of water you will not have to pay for. Yes, water will be the new oil. If you do not have one, install a fireplace or wood stove in your home now. Dry your clothing on a clothesline or at least get a clothesline and pins so you will be able to. Buy fans and use them as much as you can in place of air conditioning. If things get tough, you will have fans that can run on less power. Learn how to can, dry, and vacuum-pack foods.

- Learn to do more with less. Instead of making several trips to stores, plan an itinerary that gets the most done in one trip to save gas. Plan menus carefully to avoid throwing out leftovers, swap books and CDs with friends to save money, and close off unused rooms in your house so you do not need to heat or cool them. Remember, survival is 50 percent what you can do with and 50 percent what you can do without.

- Build your reserves. Put real needs and future needs first. The first step in building reserves is to get out of and stay out of debt. While there are some opportunities where limited, short-term borrowing is justified, you need to get on the positive side by accumulating property, assets (e.g., equipment, tools, trade goods), and life supplies in place of debts for luxuries, expendables, and services you could do for yourself.

- Think smaller. While you may be able to "live large" (e.g., big refrigerator, whole house air conditioning, big SUV, lights on in every room) today, you must have the ability to downsize your needs quickly. Electric bills and fuel bills could quickly become unaffordable. Get a smaller refrigerator. You can use it for cold drinks in summer, but it could replace your big one if things get tough. At least half of what you now keep in that big refrigerator (e.g., bread, cheese, soft drinks, water, pickles) does not need to be there. Have enough fans and small heaters to keep a few rooms comfortable if you cannot run that big furnace and air conditioning unit. Replace all your incandescent bulbs with compact fluorescents. Another benefit of these steps is that you will be able to get by better with a portable generator, solar, or wind power if the need arises. Unless you need it for business, trade in that big SUV for something smaller. If you must have that big automobile to "make a statement," you are already a victim of the system. Consider getting a bicycle for short trips in good weather. Save gas and get exercise. That's a win-win. A bicycle is also the ideal survival escape vehicle. You can carry more, move faster, and go almost anywhere, and bikes are actually more efficient than walking. The Vietcong used them to move and supply a whole army in Vietnam.

- Buy durable stuff. If you need to, spend a bit more on tools, generators, vehicles, weapons, and electronics. Do some research. When possible, buy military surplus equipment that is specifically designed for hard use and easy maintenance. Be sure to buy spare parts, tools, and manuals for all essential survival and self-reliance items. You may not be able to afford or even access a replacement part or a repair shop when you need it most.

- Stock up on essentials. Buy nonperishable or long-lasting foods (e.g., pasta, honey, sugar, vinegar, molasses, rice, cornmeal) and essential supplies, such as toilet paper, soap, toothpaste, light bulbs, batteries, LP gas cylinders, water filters, socks, underwear, ammunition, candles, clothesline and clothespins, matches, over-the-counter medications, canning equipment, how-to books, and don't forget a spare sump pump. (A Department of Defense study conducted in 1985 at Fort Detrick, Maryland, concluded that 86 percent of tested medications retained at least 90 percent of their potency for twenty to forty years. As a result, the US Food and Drug Administration has now initiated the Shelf Life Extension Program (SLEP).)

- Stock up on tradable goods. Just about any necessity bought today will be worth more later if you can safely store it. Good examples are batteries, toilet paper, ammunition, over-the-counter medications, cleaners, lubricants, disinfectants, salt, kerosene (which does not evaporate, is less flammable, and can be used for heaters and lanterns), vegetable seeds (vacuum packed), insecticide, tools, and anything that would be badly needed and hard to get. There are still lots of well-built World War II bolt-action rifles in new, like-new, or good condition (e.g., Mosin-Nagant 1938, Lee-Enfield 303, Gewehr 43) that can be had for less than $150, and ammunition is cheap and available. What will a good rifle and 500 rounds of ammunition be worth in trade to unarmed survivors in the future?

- Maintain a stock of bleach. Bleach will be essential for water purification, sanitation, and decontamination. Rotate the supply because it will lose strength over years. Soap and mouthwash for decontamination and insect repellent are other things to stock up on.

- Cut your energy needs. Buy crank-powered and solar-powered radios, lanterns, and flashlights, and any other devices that work independently of batteries or plug-in power sources.

- Take up gardening. Until the late twentieth century almost everyone raised vegetables for their own use (during World War II these gardens were called "victory gardens"). Even chicken coops were common in the city. Big lawns, swimming pools, and supermarkets became part of the lazy and dependent lifestyle after the war. It is time to turn some of that grass back into food. These would be truly "freedom gardens" or "survival gardens." You save money, eat better, and get exercise. There is no downside!

- Research solar- or wind-power systems. Generators are great for short-term emergencies, but how much fuel can you store and how much will there be in a future economy?

- Arm yourself. If you have not already done so, consider purchasing at least one firearm and at least 500 rounds of ammunition. At the very least, have a .22-caliber handgun (revolver or automatic) and a rifle of the same caliber. These will give you some deterrent against predators—animal and human. Much better, get yourself a reliable (e.g., Glock, Colt, Ruger, SIG, Smith & Wesson) 9mm, .40-caliber, or .45-caliber autoloading handgun that will stop any home invader or looter. Even if you lock up the firearms in a safe place for now, you should get them now. Their value will increase faster than just about any other investment, and when you really need them, they will be worth more than any amount of money you spend.

- Consider taking up hunting and fishing. These hobbies could have real value in tough times. Not only could fish and game supplement your own food supplies, but you can also use them as trade items. Consider also learning how to dry and smoke the meat and fish that you catch.

- Always be prepared around-the-clock for an emergency. While you can't go around carrying a pack and wearing a protective suit, you can keep items on your person, in your locker, at your desk, and in your vehicle that will give you an edge in an emergency. Wherever possible, carry a pocketknife. A good-quality single blade or the ubiquitous Swiss Army knife will be invaluable in a number of situations. Carry a folding N95 respirator in your pocket for when smoke, dust, and perhaps biological hazards fill the air. One of those tiny LED flashlights can go on your key chain. Include extra medications if you need them, as well as some painkillers and Band-Aids. Large plastic bags can become protection against rain, wind, and chemical exposure. A water-filtration straw (available at sporting goods stores) could come in handy, and a whistle may be something to consider. If concealed carry is legal and practical, a small firearm may be your choice. If not, go with a small canister of pepper spray. A more complete survival kit should be in your vehicle, briefcase, or locker. Wear sensible shoes that you could run through debris in if necessary.

- Develop alternative income sources. Don't give up your day job if you still have one, but do start to develop a backup source or sources of income. If you have skills, consider developing them into a home business. Accumulate the tools and supplies you may need to make money in a desperate economy. Auto repair, home repair, gun repair, reloading, food preservation, clothing repair, shoe repair, and many other skills will be in high demand. Gathering and rehabilitating broken and discarded appliances, tools, and furniture could be a good business. Surplus sales and the sale of survival and self-reliance products would be a good choice.

- Stay healthy. Get regular medical and dental checkups. Keep your teeth in good condition. Stock up on prescription and nonprescription medications. Have extra pairs of glasses. Once good medical care becomes unavailable or unaffordable, it will be a bad time to discover that you have a problem that could have been treated or prevented earlier. Learn first aid and stock up on such basic first-aid items as gauze pads, tape, bandages, splints, antibiotic cream, and disinfectants.

- Assemble kits, caches, plans, and packs. While "slow disasters" (e.g., climate changes, economic decline, shortages, and crime—by the criminals and the state) will challenge survival for most, "fast disasters" (e.g., riots, epidemics, floods, and storms) will be more frequent and more devastating in many areas. With less and less help available, it will be critical for every household to have the capacity to sustain itself for weeks or even months without outside sources of water, food, sanitation services, heat, and power, or even police, fire, and medical services. In addition, each person (including children) should have a survival pack that is light enough to carry but contains all the necessities (necessities only) to survive in any weather for several days in the event that you are forced to evacuate. There should be a small quantity of water and a water filtration device, nonperishable foods, shelter and warmth (e.g., sleeping bag, blanket, tent, plastic sheets), a first-aid kit, spare socks, underwear, medications, weapons, fire starters, a knife, and everything you would need. There are many sources of lists on how to put together a survival pack, but don't wait. Any pack is better than no pack.

- Coordinate emergency plans. Consider what I have said about the future. Consider the various emergencies (e.g., fire, assault, flood, epidemic) that could happen in your area. Think "what if?" Make basic plans for each situation. Think, "If this happens, I will do this." Consider what skills and supplies you need, with whom you can work, priorities, primary and alternate evacuation routes, and communications. When others (family and friends) are involved, passwords and rendezvous locations are necessary. Remember that many emergency situations may develop while you are not at home or while you are asleep. Where will you be? Where will your loved ones be? If you are one of those people who think, "I don't want to think about it," then you are already a victim, and so are those you are responsible for.

- Network and team up. There are a lot more self-reliance, self-defense, survival-oriented people out there than is generally visible. The media and government officials generally discourage independence and self-reliance. Practitioners are often low profile and disinclined to share their ideas with others. Even though self-reliance is essential, family, community, and group support (not dependence) is critical to long-term survival, greatly enhanced potential, and recovery. Self-reliance does not require isolation. Self-reliance means you have a choice as to whom you support, when, and how, as well as how you are supported by others. In the short term, the capacity *for* individual self-reliance is critical. In the long term, the option and capacity exist for mutual voluntary support.

- Teach children to become self-reliant and to value freedom. A recent study indicated that many young people become stressed if they lose their cell phones. They are no longer individuals; they think and act as part of a network of cell phones and websites. They may confuse reality with computer games. Their grasp of history is so shallow that they are truly "doomed to repeat" the errors that ruined and enslaved past societies. It is the most important parental responsibility to ensure that their children have the will, knowledge, and capability of taking care of themselves in emergencies and through hard times. The cruelest thing you can do to your children and grandchildren is to set them up for disaster by overprotecting and underpreparing them. It is the duty of every responsible parent to empower children with a sense of self-reliance and independence. This is the gift of life and freedom.

- Use technology but do not become dependent on it. The Internet, computers, and cell phones are great tools for gathering information, networking, communicating, ordering equipment and books, and making some extra money, but these tools will be the first to fail or be used against you when you need them most. So use them, but don't need them. Keep hard copies (e.g., books, papers, tapes) in a safe place. Develop direct communication systems based on those used by the underground and spycraft of the pre-computer age. Set up things so that, at any point, things (e.g., emergency plans, organizations, teams, and business) can go on without regular communication.

- Don't let down your guard. The recent Supreme Court decision to support at least part of the Second Amendment, a temporary drop in the price of oil, or a slightly improved economy does not mean that all will be well. The United Nations wants to ban small arms on an international scale and override the US Constitution. The weakening dollar guarantees that fuel and everything else but your paycheck will go up as your living standard goes down. Those in power will use every trick to disarm you and render you poor and dependent. You *will* have to fight for your freedoms and struggle for survival. Hold on when you must. Advance when you can. Know your friends and your enemies.

- Build up a self-reliance library. There is lots of great, free information on virtually every survival and self-reliance subject available on the Internet. Google "survival," "self-reliance," "self-defense," "water purification," "first aid," and other survival-related terms. Print what you find and make binders that you keep in secure containers. When things get tough, you may not be able to access the Internet, so print it now.

- Don't give up and don't doubt yourself. Those who live in challenging times have the opportunity to make a profound difference in the future. You will be the ones who decide if your children and grandchildren survive to be free, creative, and happy.

CONCLUSION

Live Free USA has been fighting for freedom and self-reliance for more than forty years. We have seen the threats of the Soviet Union, Red Dawn, Y2K, and many others come and go. We have also seen a lot of panic peddling by various groups trying to promote products or sell fear and hate. We have seen dozens of so-called survival organizations come and go. We have never been a big organization, and we have never received a large contribution or grant, but we have endured and retained a reputation for responsibility and integrity. We have never claimed to know exactly what will happen, when it will happen, or who to blame. What we do know is that changes and disasters will happen, and will happen to many of you.

We also know that only through emergency preparedness, self-reliance, and a steadfast determination to hold on to every inch of personal freedom and survival capability is there any hope for the future. If you have not seriously thought about changing your life-style to a prepared, self-reliant, freedom-first mode, do it before it's too late. If you already call yourself a "survivalist" or a "self-reliance practitioner," redouble your efforts and reach out to friends and neighbors now.

If you do not happen to things, things will happen to you. You can happen to the future before it happens, or you can choose to be a future victim.

2

Self-Reliance Overview

There is no question that the next decades will be dangerous to our lives and freedoms, but how we respond and adjust will determine the future of America. What we do now to expand and support the movement will make the difference between a freer and more self-reliant society and a more centralized and oppressive one.

While self-reliance is often treated as simply a form of advanced survival preparedness, it is different in both psychology and execution. Preparing and surviving imply that one is anticipating a passing threat to life, or life as we know it, that must be survived in order to recover and rebuild as life was before the event. In this respect prepping may be compared to a life raft that saves life but has no sail or destination. While survival is certainly a laudable and necessary objective and preparedness is essential to getting through the multiplying threats of the twenty-first century, it will not take us to a new and better place. In fact, mere survival leaves us alive among the ruins and with little control of where we land. True practical self-reliance goes beyond survival in the following ways:

- It immediately changes how we live and provides economic and psychological advantages over the unprepared and dependent masses.

- It is proactive rather than reactive. Instead of hoping to get through coming challenges, you are challenging current and future threats.

- It is positive and inspiring. While the populace may be in denial about impending disasters and negative trends, people more readily embrace ideas that make them more independent, secure, and prosperous.

- The focus is not just on staying alive. Self-reliance is about being better, smarter, and safer, and going toward the future with confidence.

- For those who want change, self-reliance offers a revolutionary opportunity to withdraw taxable income, avoids regulatory systems, and counters centralized power in a positive and nonviolent movement.

True self-reliance then can be compared to a ship that not only keeps you afloat, but also takes you to a better place. Self-reliance advocates should have a firm concept of where that ship is going. We also need to face the fact that those who have benefitted from centralized authority, dependence on the grid, and massive taxation will act strongly to intimidate, discourage, and misrepresent self-reliance practices and advocates. Such resistance may become violent. As the existing economic, political, and support systems fail, the conflict may take on aggressive dimensions.

All this must take into account the underlying imperatives of surviving the assaults of nature (e.g., storms, epidemics, climate change) and mankind (e.g., resource depletion, famine, or war) that will ravage future decades. It is far better to put ourselves and our posterity aboard the ship of self-reliance than the life raft of preparedness. Conceding, of course, that the ship still needs to have life rafts aboard.

We must not regard self-reliance as simply a technical process for sustaining life needs into the future. Our children deserve better than maintenance. They deserve to come out of the challenges of survival and change as smarter, freer, and more human. Self-reliance is not about going back. Self-reliance is about building a better future as the failed and wrong values decline and fall.

UNITED AS INDIVIDUALS

Humans are social by nature. Survival skills and self-reliance capabilities may keep us alive alone for a while, but we are hardly human without family, friends, and associations. The struggles to survive, find water, build shelter, gather food, and defend against others leave no time for thinking, improving, or advancing. Effective self-reliance is being independent while choosing to share and exchange with others. Being basically self-reliant provides the foundation for voluntary participation in cooperative efforts and exchanges.

One may have special skills or excessive supplies in one area but be short in others. A small family or community may be vulnerable to looters or need help producing food. The difference between collectivist and centralized society and self-reliance is that the power of choices starts at the bottom with the individual and family instead of with bureaucrats. As we develop individual and family self-reliance capacity, we should be creating regional and dispersed networks for both technological and political support. If self-reliance is a ship and not just a life raft, then we will need a fleet to get through the storms ahead.

German philosopher George Hegel (1770–1831) developed the theory of the dialectic. He postulated that there is a flow of events and changes from one time to the next that is driven by multiple events and conditions. Karl Marx wrongly used the dialectic theory to show history leading only to a communist society. As we examine history leading from the times of the American Revolution through the twentieth century, it is hard to avoid the evidence of a continual dialectic flow from one decade to the next. The following three phases of change will not actually happen as distinct periods; they will overlap and occur concurrently in some ways. All three of them are in progress now; however the effects of the second and third phases are less evident, as not enough time has passed to make their full effects known.

Phase 1

- Economic instability.
- Loss of public confidence and support.
- Frequent regional disasters with less and less recovery.
- Degradation of big, centralized business, government, and infrastructure.
- Rise of minority preparedness and self-reliance culture.
- Rise in small self-reliance technologies.

Phase 2

- Disintegration of established economic systems and bureaucracies.
- Shortages of life-critical materials and services.
- Unrecoverable disasters (e.g., epidemics, storms, droughts) that significantly reduce populations and render areas uninhabitable.
- Unrest and conflicts within society and between nations caused by shortages and limited resources.
- Extremist leaders within and outside government will feed on public fear and desperation to accumulate power and wealth at the expense of the public.
- Desperate actions by governments to retain control and wealth may include confiscations, suspension of liberties, and general oppression. The prepared and self-reliant may be branded as selfish and dangerous.[1]

---

1   If self-reliance is still a small minority movement at this stage, it will probably be extinguished. Freedom and self-reliance will only survive if they have been advocated and organized, and have taken root in communities.

- Ideally, self-reliance businesses, organizations, and concepts will begin to involve a significant portion of the public.

Phase 3

- Through evolution or revolution, government will be reinvented as a more limited, decentralized, and supportive entity.
- The primary economic and political power will come from the countries and states driven by a highly independent populace.
- Multifunction networks of families, communities, and organizations will provide life-critical materials and support to semi-self-reliant people.[2]

DECLARING INDEPENDENCE THROUGH PRACTICAL SELF-RELIANCE

The table below is a very brief outline of a family plan for replacement or backup systems for supplies and services currently provided by the failing centralized structures. Don't let the image of doomsday prepping, "off-the-grid" capabilities discourage you from working toward reasonable and responsible self-reliance in all the categories.

---

2 Ultimately, we will need to do many things cooperatively. Long-term self-reliance requires almost all of an individual's and a family's time and energy. This leaves little for improvement, learning, and progress. If a community floods, its people can all build multiple sandbag dikes around each house or can work together to build one effective dike at the river. If a gang attacks a community, families will be killed off one by one unless they all work together.

CATEGORY	ACTION OUTLINE
WATER	NOW: Store at least ten gallons per person; have bleach available; acquire a good-quality filter system. FUTURE: Install rain barrels, cistern, advanced filters. ISSUES: Droughts, waterborne infections, legal issues.
FOOD PRODUCTION	NOW: Start gardening; stock up on heirloom seeds; take up fishing and hunting. FUTURE: Enlarge garden, consider aquaponics. ISSUES: Climate change, available area, security.
FOOD PRESERVATION	NOW: Store at least thirty to ninety days' supply. FUTURE: Canning, drying, smoking. ISSUES: Supplies, storage space.
SHELTER	NOW: Home preparedness and safety; alternative shelter for evacuation. FUTURE: Develop home as base for meeting all life-critical needs. ISSUES: Ownership, community compatibility.
HEALTH	NOW: Maintain and improve while you can! Stop bad habits; exercise regularly. FUTURE: Ability to avoid exposure to public is critical; clean water and adequate food must be maintained. ISSUES: Poor sanitation, government interference.

SANITATION	NOW: Chemical toilets; bleach; stock up on toilet paper. FUTURE: Outhouses, lime, ash, bleach, composting toilets. ISSUES: Legal issues.
MEDICAL CARE	NOW: Learn first aid; stock supplies and medications. FUTURE: Develop capacity for advanced and extended medical care; learn alternative medicines; network with medically skilled personnel. ISSUES: Medication acquisition and storage, legal issues.
PERSONAL HYGIENE	NOW: Improve health habits; stock up on soap, Listerine, alcohol, bleach, toothpaste. FUTURE: Learn to make soap; install showers without water pressure. ISSUES: Water supply, drainage.
LAUNDRY	NOW: Changes of clothes; stock up on soap and detergent. FUTURE: Laundry tubs, wringers, scrubboards, clotheslines. ISSUES: Water supply, drainage.
HEATING	NOW: LP gas heaters, sleeping bags, tent in house. FUTURE: Wood stoves, closed rooms. ISSUES: Safety, fire, carbon monoxide, fuel supplies.

TRANSPORTATION	NOW: Alternatives to driving in an emergency; evacuation packs; bicycles. FUTURE: Bicycles, electric vehicles. ISSUES: Range and weight limits, routes.
CLOTHING	NOW: Plenty but stock up on socks, underwear, sewing supplies. FUTURE: Manual sewing machine; learn to knit and repair. ISSUES: Skills, supplies, tools.
WASTE DISPOSAL	NOW: Temporary health hazard; bleach; insect spray; burning. FUTURE: Fewer wastes; burn for fuel; use for compost.
COOKING	NOW: Have camp stoves. FUTURE: Solar ovens, rocket stoves, outdoor cooking. ISSUES: Safety, fire, carbon monoxide, fuel supplies.
ENERGY	NOW: Batteries, generators. FUTURE: Supplemental and alternative solar and wind. Need reduction. ISSUES: Space for systems, safety, legal.
FIRE SUPPRESSION	NOW: Fire extinguishers, smoke/CO detectors, and ability to evacuate and survive. FUTURE: Large volume water pumps. Community cooperation, prevention. ISSUES: Increased risks, heat and embers from adjoining areas.

PERSONAL DEFENSE	NOW: Personal weapons and vigilance; stock up on ammunition, parts. FUTURE: Increased need for more effective weapons; need for family or community round-the-clock vigilance and defense. ISSUES: Legal issues.
TRADE/BARTER	NOW: Trade and barter when possible; stock up on barter items; learn tradable skills. FUTURE: Value in hard items and skills replaces currency in many areas. ISSUES: Legal and tax issues.
TOOLS	NOW: In addition to packable survival tools, have tools for home repair, and rescue. FUTURE: Shop tools, garden tools, auto tools, nails, screws and fasteners are all valuable. Replace power tools with hand tools, use solar power to recharge cordless drills. ISSUES: Cost, storage space, skill in use.
MISCELLANEOUS CHALLENGES NUCLEAR, BIOLOGICAL	NOW: Carry N-95 masks and hand cleaner; avoid crowds. FUTURE: Get out of contaminated area ASAP; don protective wear and dust mask; remove contaminated clothing and decontaminate ASAP; treat symptoms, dehydration. ISSUES: Shelter, radiation sickness, epidemics.

Preparedness is about surviving the future. Self-reliance is, or should be, about conquering the future. Preparedness is about reacting to events. Self-reliance is about being events. Both preparedness and self-reliance are necessary, but survival alone cannot be enough. A smarter, freer, more responsible, and self-reliant people must be determined to own the future regardless of the dangers and challenges that lie ahead.

3

Water: The Foundation of Self-Reliance

"Water, water everywhere, nor any drop to drink" was the lament of Cooleridge's Ancient Mariner, becalmed and thirsty in a sea of undrinkable saltwater. Today water comes from a faucet or is purchased in bottles, clean and (arguably) pure. But what if it doesn't?

A BRIEF HISTORY OF WATER

Since water is essential to life and agriculture, all early civilizations developed along rivers or near springs and lakes. Ultimately the great cities developed around these water sources. Human waste polluted these same waters, resulting in frequent plagues that tended to keep the populations regulated. While those in outlying areas used water from safe wells and springs, the water in populated areas was always hazardous. Beer, wine, and boiled teas were safe alternatives.

A whole branch of my family was wiped out in the 1800s from a polluted well. Pumped water supplies to cities were introduced in the early 1800s and came right out of the same polluted rivers or lakes with or without chlorination. Chicago's South Side did not get filtration until the late 1940s. On a stormy day the tap water would be a bit cloudy and smelled of chlorine. A minnow got through once in a while.

So cheap, safe tap water is a fairly recent innovation. Any extended interruption of this supply would result in chaos and a great reduction in the population through disease, thirst, and violence. The survivors would be those who could effectively apply the methods used in previous centuries.

THE LIFE ESSENTIAL NEED

Next to air, water is the most critical life-sustaining substance. The human body can survive much, much longer without food than without water. In the long term, you can't even produce and cook most foods without access to water. Your cleaning, decontamination, first aid, sanitation, and fire control also depend on water. Wars have been fought over access to water sources, and whole cultures have risen and fallen with the flow of rivers and springs. Water supplies are major targets for terrorists and are vulnerable to all manner of natural and man-made disaster. Not only will safe water be critical to your family's survival, it could be a more valuable trade commodity than food or medicine. The water pumps are the heart of urban/suburban civilization, and without them, they would die in a matter of days. Compared to water, oil is hardly significant. Truly, he who controls the water controls life, and he who has his own water is free.

Depending on age, health, and level of activity and environmental factors (e.g., temperature and humidity), the average person can only survive about three days without water. The average person under normal conditions requires at least one quart of drinking water per day. When reasonable sanitation and cooking needs are added, a half-gallon per day is a good rule of thumb for emergency storage. If you have elected to store quantities of dehydrated foods, you need to remember to store more water for rehydration. For our purposes here, we will classify water as:

- Stored: drinkable water that is deliberately stored for emergency use.
- Available: water that may be in or near your home but is not generally thought of, or stored for, emergency uses.
- Accessible: water that can be accessed or gathered for use in emergencies.

Use some common sense. During the Gulf War, people suffocated to death in improperly used gas masks rather than breathe air that *might* be contaminated. If you are very thirsty and have no prospect of safe water being available soon, you should drink the safest water you have even if it's not 100 percent certified clean. Unless you *know* it's poisoned or contains a fatal contaminant, do the best you can (if anything) to purify it and drink it.

Never ration water. Water is better in the body than in the bottle. There is no long-term advantage to being thirsty. Yes, you may run out of stored water sooner, but that water will be in your body doing its job. You should conserve the water stored in you. Obviously, avoid sweating if possible and never mop it away. Do not consume caffeinated or alcoholic beverages that increase urination and actually take water out of the body.

Stored Water

While in theory you can never store too much water, it is heavy and takes up a lot of room. Sorry, there is no such thing as dehydrated water. If you anticipate that you will be staying at home and that your home will be safe from fire, floods, or other disasters, then you can store your water there. If, however, your home could be damaged or inaccessible, you should consider storing water in a safer but reachable location. Consider whether you may need to carry your water. A fifty-five-gallon drum of water in your basement would be of no use if you have to evacuate.

Plastic containers that were designed to hold water, juice, or soft drinks are good for storing water. Milk containers can be used but are flimsy and hard to get clean. Never use containers that originally held soaps, solvents, or other chemicals. Containers should be rinsed thoroughly with clean water and then soaked in a mild (10 percent) bleach solution. As soon as you dump the solution out, fill the container with clean water and seal tightly.

Most municipal waters can be stored without additional treatment. If you are storing well water or other water you are unsure of, add four or five drops of household bleach to each gallon. Of course, you may simply want to buy bottled water at the store. Five gallons of stored water per person should be sufficient for most basic emergencies.

Typical Amish home with all roof water directed to a cistern in the basement. The water is then pumped up to the kitchen sink with a hand pump.

Rain barrels catching rain from a garage roof. A PVC pipe and valve system connects the barrels to supply water to a garden. A small pump could add pressure and pump to the house. One half-inch of rain on a 20 x 20-foot roof area provides more than one hundred gallons of water. Bird droppings and other roof residue make filtration and/or bleach or boiling necessary for drinking.

If you have an early warning that there may be a water shortage, you should collect as much water as possible while it is still flowing. Fill your bathtub, sinks, pans, and other containers. Fill your washing machine (but do not add soap) as well as any children's wading pools and tote bins that may be available.

Available Water

If you have failed to store enough water or you find yourself in a location where no stored water is available, you may need to use water from other sources. Not all of these sources will be drinkable, but they may provide water for other needs. If you have your own well, you have the water problem solved if you have a backup power supply for the pump. If not, get one! The toilet flush tank (not the bowl) contains several gallons of clean drinkable water. Do not flush the toilet with this clean water! Scoop it out and use it for drinking and cooking. You can flush the toilet with used, dirty brown water from washing or with water that is unsafe for drinking anyway.

Your water heater has water. Turn off the main water valves and gas and drain the twenty to sixty gallons of good water from the tank. Water pipes in a building contain gallons of water after the supply has stopped. Turn off the main valve to prevent drain-back and contamination, and drain the system from the lowest faucet. This is usually the laundry room sink.

Swimming pools and garden ponds can hold hundreds of gallons of usable water. In fact, they may be considered as family emergency water reservoirs. Properly maintained swimming pool water may be used for drinking and cooking, but the chlorine content will affect taste. Even a small pool will supply lots of water for cleaning and flushing. If left uncovered, it can be contaminated with airborne biological, chemical, and radioactive materials. Maintaining a rolling boil for thirty minutes can kill most biological contaminants. Nuclear fallout can be removed through filtration. Decorative garden ponds may contain debris, animal and bird feces, and other contaminants, and would require filtration and bleach treatment or boiling before use.

Many homes have a sump pump and a sump pit in the basement to pump away ground water seepage before it can flood the basement. Ground water is not well water and is often contaminated. A prudent homeowner would have a battery-powered backup pump or a generator to ensure that this pump will run during a power outage. Assuming that if your city water supply is gone, so is your electricity, you will need to pump or bail out this water regularly. This can be a supply of water for flushing, cleaning, or watering plants. As a last resort you could filter, bleach, or boil this water for drinking.

Accessible Water

In the old days people had gutters running to rain barrels to gather water for home use. Large plantations had cisterns to collect rainwater in the wet months for use in the dry times. Rain on a house roof in one storm can provide enough water for weeks. Even dew and frost melting into the gutters can produce several quarts of water each morning. Consider having the necessary gutter piping to divert this water into containers. The water will be contaminated but can be filtered, bleached, or boiled for use and drinking.

Rivers and streams today are almost always contaminated. Even in wilderness areas, animal feces and carcasses upstream may pollute the seemingly clean water. Consider open streams and drainage ditches as a last resort. As is, water from those sources can be used for watering plants and fire protection. If you have no other alternative, you can filter, bleach, or boil it for washing and drinking. Beware of water sources that have no plants growing near them, have odd smells or colorations, or near which you see dead animals. These sources may contain manmade or natural (e.g., arsenic) contamination that cannot be easily removed.

Mopping up the morning dew from rocks and metal surfaces (e.g., cars, boats) with sponges or rags and wringing it into a pan can gather a considerable amount of water. Water trapped in soil and mud can be placed in cloth or a clean sock and squeezed out.

The so-called "desert still" was designed to distill small amounts of water from seemingly dry desert soil and cactus pieces in an emergency. This same system can be used to distill much more water from moist soil and foliage. A similar still can be constructed to render drinkable water from saltwater as illustrated below right.

Most plants transpirate (sweat) water every day. Wrapping plastic bags around heavy hanging foliage will collect this water in the low corner of the bag.

Wringing water out of mud.

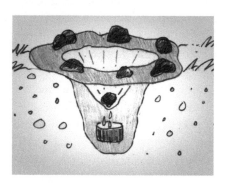

"Desert still" consists of a hole about fifteen to twenty inches deep and eighteen to twenty-four inches in diameter. A water collection cup or pan is placed in the bottom along with any available plant material. A clear sheet of plastic is suspended with slack over the hole and held in place with rocks. A small rock is placed in the center to create a low center point. As the sun heats the hole, water gathers on the inside of the plastic, runs down, and drips into the cup. In the evening, remove the cup of safe water.

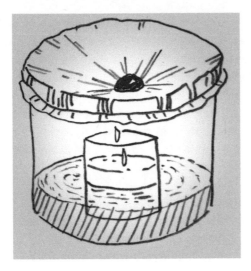

A solar simple still made from a round pan and clear plastic. Place a weighted (so it won't float) cup in the center and saltwater in the pan. The sun will distill the water into the cup without the salt.

Now that you have water, you need to know how to filter it, purify it, and conserve it.

Filtration

The filtration of visible (muddy, murky) gross contaminants can be accomplished using such items as coffee filters, clean cloth, or clean sand. This does not make the water safe to drink. You must boil and treat the water before it is safe. Cartridge filters are designed to remove virtually all biological, chemical and particulate contamination from water. Most camping and outdoor sports stores sell these units for $30 to $60. These units are portable and can filter hundreds of gallons of water per filter. You simply must have several of these.

Homemade water filter using alternating layers of sand and charcoal separated by coffee filters. Note charcoal, sand, and bleach on top of rain barrel.

Distillation

Boiling water into steam and then condensing it into clean water provides water free of biological and particulate contaminants, but some volatile chemical contaminants can remain with the distilled water. Distilled water often tastes flat. Shaking it to aerate will restore a normal water taste. Stills can be improvised, but having the components ready and tested is better yet. A still system (seen at the bottom of this page) consists of the following:

1. A heat source, such as a stove or fire.
2. A closed tank or pot in which to boil the contaminated water.
3. A long tube or coil to take the steam away and cool it.
4. The tub can be cooled by air (coiling) or water. Wrap the coil in a cloth kept wet.
5. A container to catch the water.

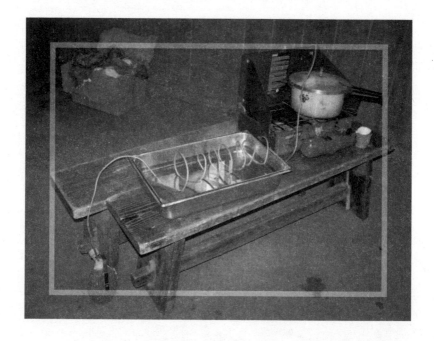

Improvised distillation system using a camp stove, copper tubing, and a pan of water to cool the steam back to water.

Treatment

When other methods are unavailable, water can be made safe through boiling or treating with chemicals. Bringing water to a rolling boil for three to five minutes will kill all biological contaminants and drive off many volatile chemicals. Filtering it through a coffee filter will remove most particulates.

In general eight to ten drops of household bleach (8 percent chlorine) per gallon will kill biological contaminants. Ten drops of tincture of iodine (USPA 2 percent) will do the job as well. Use up to sixteen drops of bleach or twelve drops of iodine for severely polluted water. Mix in the bleach or iodine and let it stand for an hour before drinking.

Water-purification tablets are available from camping supply outlets for about five dollars for a fifty-tablet bottle. These are very small bottles that can be carried in pockets and survival kits.

Conservation

Water that is unsafe to drink may be fine for washing clothes or watering plants. Water that has been used for washing or is from an unsafe source can still be used to flush the toilet. Try not to use drinking water for anything but drinking, washing food and hands, and providing medical care.

CONCLUSION

Next to air, water is the single-most important ingredient for the preservation of life and civilization. The survivor must have stored water and the capacity to filter additional water to get through short- and medium-term emergencies. True self-reliance requires the development of a variety of water-gathering and -purifying skills and systems. Clean water will be a commodity far more valuable than gold, oil, or even food under some scenarios.

4

Food for the Long Haul

Obviously if you have not stored enough food to get you through a short emergency, you won't be around to cope with food shortages lasting years or decades into the future. There are many books on the subject of food storage for "disasters." I have written many articles on that subject as well. Here we will consider the implications of permanent or very long-term food shortages. Such food shortages could develop slowly as prices go up and availability declines or rather suddenly after an economic collapse, epidemic, or biological disaster. At some point, reserves would run out and even preppers' stocks would be depleted.

A SHORT HISTORY OF FOOD

It could be said that the whole history of mankind has revolved around food and water. Our hunter-gatherer ancestors took hundreds of thousands of years to develop hunting and foraging skills and finally to become fishermen, herders, and farmers. Until the twentieth century, the great majority of the population was employed in some aspect of food production and processing. Planting, harvesting, raising and butchering livestock, canning, and drying were practiced, or at least understood, by virtually everyone. Early cities were marketplaces for food, and their size was limited by how many could be fed by surrounding farms and pastures. Farms were generally small and self-sufficient. Farmers tended to grow a variety of crops to ship directly to nearby markets. Railroads facilitated vastly expanded urban areas while machines made it possible for a few to feed many. Farmers started growing huge fields of just one or two "hybrid" crops.

After World War II, supermarkets supplied by trucks replaced grocery stores, butcher shops, bakeries, and greengrocers of the past. Prepackaged foods and fast-food restaurants virtually eliminated cooking for most families. Today we have a highly complex and vulnerable food production and distribution system feeding a highly concentrated and dependent population. Every aspect of food production, processing, and distribution is dependent on petroleum and natural gas. Climate change, along with decades of overuse, has depleted water supplies until they are nearly exhausted in many areas. Artificial government subsidies and policies have created unsustainable false production and supply systems. As water becomes less available and fuel becomes more and more expensive, the availability of affordable foods will start to decline. These effects will hit the third world first as the United States stops exporting foods. This will devastate our trade balance and create inflation. Restaurants will be the first to be hit as people return to cooking more at home. The first signs of these trends are already evident.

CHALLENGES AND SOLUTIONS

Fortunately, most areas of the United States have the potential to feed their populations. The exceptions are those cities in desert areas—such as Nevada, Arizona, and New Mexico—that have expanded populations far beyond the capacity of the immediate area to feed them. Highly concentrated multi-urban areas throughout the world that are dependent on massive supplies of food hauled in from thousands of miles cannot be sustained and will depopulate through attrition, epidemics, disorder, and migration to a sustainable level. The surviving suburban, rural, and small-town populations will be forced to adapt to a new normal in regard to food supplies. Menus will be driven more by season and region. Things like fresh orange juice and ocean fish may be harder (or impossible) to come by in the Midwest. Dried fruits and preserves may be the main vitamin C source during the winter months. Sugar and sugary foods will be reduced by unavailability, not regulations. Home farms and sharecropping may return. Farming will return to smaller, more intensive, and less machine- and chemical-dependent methods.

Baking shed, smokehouse, and drying shed at a typical Amish homestead. Food preservation and preparation may become a major home activity again in the future.

Rationing, Black Market, and Price Controls

During World War II, many things were rationed: milk, butter, vegetable oil, cheese, flour, rice, sugar, and meat. This list may give a hint about what food items would be in short supply first. Fruits from the south and any foods from overseas were practically nonexistent. Anyone who had a yard had a victory garden to supplement groceries. Lots of folks in town kept chickens for eggs, and fruit trees (e.g., apples, peaches) were pretty common. Excursions to nearby farms were common, as were farmers coming into cities selling vegetables and eggs off trucks and wagons.

You could have gotten additional food at high prices from black-market suppliers, but this was viewed as unpatriotic or even treasonous. The failure of the communist collective system in the old Soviet Union made home gardens and the black market the primary working food supply system for over fifty years. Price controls have been tried as a method of making food affordable in the past. The results have always been catastrophic. The government cannot produce or manage food supplies. When it does, true prices go up, supplies go down, and black market cartels grow. Nevertheless, we can anticipate these various strategies to be introduced as situations deteriorate.

If you can't believe that food was ever rationed in the United States, look no further than the ration stamps and ration book in this image that were issued here during World War II.

Foraging

Foraging can include walking the woodlands for edible plants as well as rummaging about in abandoned stores for remaining food items. It does not include raiding farm fields and gardens or looting stores and homes. Hunger can inspire desperate acts. There may be times when feeding loved ones will justify actions that would not be ethical under "normal" conditions. Keep in mind that this kind of "foraging" can cost you your life—and that you may be the victim of desperate foragers yourself. Defense is always stronger than offense, and preparedness is always more ethical than desperation. Being able to survive on foods you have stored and are producing puts you on much stronger ethical and tactical ground. As for wild edible foraging, it may be helpful foraging for "weeds" as a supplement in the early stages of farming, but the woodland around populated areas will quickly be denuded of edibles (and firewood) by other foragers.

Purslane (left; Wikipedia / Zoo Fair) and plantain (right; Wikipedia/Jesse Taylor) are two very common "weeds" that are edible. Many more are available in lots, woods, and marshes.

Hunting and Trapping

Hunters have a great advantage in the early stages of a food shortage. Restrictions will be irrelevant, and their experience at hunting and preservation of game will allow them to stock up on venison and other meats. The problem is that areas will quickly be overhunted and game will be hard to find after two or three years. The other hazard is that many will try hunting with no experience, making the woods and marshes very dangerous. Desperate people may even target hunters to try to take their kills away. Hunting will not be a recreational "sport"; it will be a serious and hazardous operation.

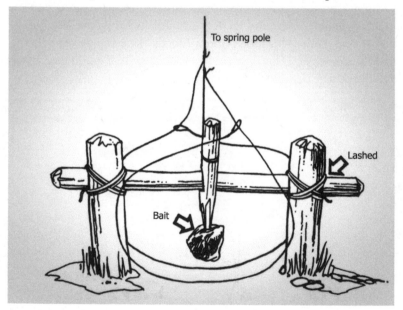

An improvised animal trap. There are many more designs to be found in outdoor survival books.

You definitely want to invest in a .22-caliber rifle for small-game hunting. This will allow you to hunt small game at the minimum cost and noise. You will want to save your larger-caliber rifle ammunition and shotgun shells for bigger game and (if necessary) self-defense. Consider putting a telescopic sight on your rifle to ensure accurate hits at longer range. You may want to consider archery, crossbows, and even slingshots for silent hunting.

Trapping requires considerable skill and practice. With everyone thrashing about in the woods, it may be ineffective, but you should know how to improvise simple traps to supplement your hunting efforts.

Fishing

Fishing has been a lifesaver in many historic famines. In the past it was impossible to overfish a lake or stream as human populations were too sparse and fishing methods were too primitive. In a future famine, most small lakes and rivers would be fished out quickly. Only the oceans would sustain a constant supply of food. In fact, once the large commercial fishing operations decline, individual fishing would improve.

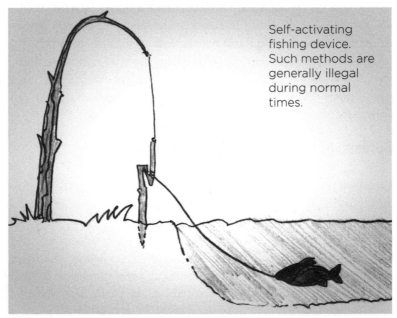

Self-activating fishing device. Such methods are generally illegal during normal times.

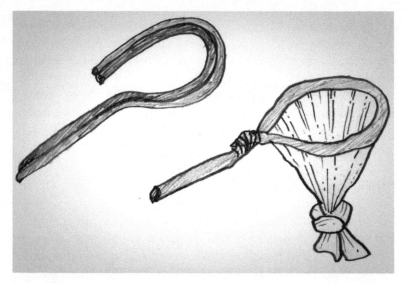

Improvised dip net using cheesecloth or other mesh material.

Knowing how to preserve fish through drying, smoking, and salting will be an important skill for the fisherman. There will be no "catch and release" in these conditions, and probably no freezer either. Consider fish traps and nets as well as poles. Remember, this is not "sport fishing." Anyone with a boat has a tremendous advantage. If you do not have a boat, you may want to consider adding a good-quality rubber raft to your emergency equipment. These can have many survival uses.

Gardening: Land, Seeds, Fertilizer, Tools

Establishing a vegetable garden is a healthy hobby that can save money during normal times and provide essential food during emergencies. Small space, raised-bed gardening is the most efficient way to grow food in the limited area of a suburban lot. Seeds, garden tools, and other supplies will not be available once things get bad, so you must start practicing gardening early and build up extra supplies to expand your garden as conditions worsen. Seeds will be particularly valuable and hard to get. Stock up on nonhybrid seeds and vacuum-package them. Invest in good hand garden tools that will last. Don't overlook the water situation. You may not have running water. Set up rain barrels and cisterns to store rain and snowmelt water. Stock up on fertilizers while you can but establish a mulch system to process waste into fertilizers. There are lots of vegetables that can be canned and dried, but consider carrots, beets, turnips, and other in-ground vegetables that can be stored in a "root cellar" type of cool, dark environment without further preserving. These staples can provide food throughout the whole winter.

Raised beds ready for planting vegetables. Notice the all-around wire fencing to keep animals out.

Aquaponics

Aquaponics is a system for food production using a closed-loop cycle where fish in tanks supply the nutrients for plants growing in soil-free beds.

The plants grow in long trays, usually made from PVC gutter pipe. In place of soil, there are beds of small glass beads that hold the roots in place and let the nourishing water from the fish tanks flow through it. The nutrients from the fish's waste fertilize the plants, and the plants filter the water as it returns to the fish tanks. While the fish need no light, the plants need to be supplied with natural or artificial light. Solar panels can supply enough power for the pumps and (if necessary) lights.

This small aquaponics system places the plants above the fish tank. A grow light and small pump would complete the system. Photos courtesy of Friendly Aquaponics.

Of course, the fish are also food and can be harvested as they grow larger. Our host facility was using tilapia and growing lettuce, sprouts, and other greens for local restaurants. The only input was food for the fish and solar energy—both of them were free from nature. Of course it's not quite as simple as that. Certain bacteria have to be introduced into the water and balances of naturally produced chemicals—such as ammonia, nitrogen, and nitrates—need to be managed to prevent toxicity to fish and plants. In this system about one gallon of water can support about one square foot of plant beds and one pound of fish stock. This methodology has great advantages for the truly self-reliant family of the future. A large closet-sized system can significantly increase food supplies to an urban-bound family. A shed, garage, or basement system could supply 100 percent of fish and vegetable needs for a small family and provide enough to trade.

Livestock

Raising chickens, ducks, and rabbits can supply important foods and trade items. Doing so may be prohibited by local ordinances, but these will change or be ignored under future food-shortage conditions.

Barter and Trade

During the German siege of Leningrad (now St. Petersburg) in 1942, the population traded valuables of all sorts to farmers in the surrounding area for turnips, beets, potatoes, and cabbages. The farmers were supposed to turn in their crops to the state, but they usually withheld some for their own families and for trade. The problem here is that the hungry farmers soon lost interest in trading food for anything. A diamond necklace might get you a few turnips, but no farmer was going to let his family be hungry for "worthless" jewelry. Gold and silver are not edible or valuable in a famine economy. However, labor to plant, guard, weed, harvest, and process the crops

Typical food drying shed using a small stove to provide heat.
Electric food dryers may not always be available.

when fuel is not available is a valuable commodity. This may be your
best trade item for food.

Remote Seeding

Before there was formal farming, ancient man would plant seeds
in good locations and let nature do the rest. He would continue
his nomadic hunting and return to the area in the fall to harvest
whatever had grown. American Indians did the same thing. In fact,
illegal marijuana growers plant their crops throughout our national

parks today. Sometimes their crops are left to hide in plain sight, but sometimes armed "campers" guard them. These methods could be employed again to grow food in more remote forests and marshes.

Critical Supplies

Things you will need to stock to make the transition to self-sufficiency include seeds, salt, seasonings, sugar, vinegar, fertilizer, and canning jars.

CONCLUSIONS

Once the false values of civilization are stripped away, food, water, and energy are the only true essentials. Water and energy are natural resources, but food must be found, produced, and preserved. There are many ways for the knowledgeable and prepared survivor to procure and produce foods. While food production may be more challenging in urban and suburban areas, those who master the techniques and are able to feed their families will be the foundation of the new communities. Family, community, and group food trade and support systems will be critical as shortages and rationing develop. Once the would-be survivor gets past "prepping" for short-term food emergencies, he must consider developing long-term food self-sufficiency.

5

Food, Famine, and Power

I don't write much about food for survival. That's because it is so well covered by thousands of articles and books. Next to air and water, food is the most important survival necessity. Most healthy people can get by without much food for several weeks or longer. Most homes have a few weeks' worth of food around, and most areas have additional food available on store shelves or in the lakes and forests. Of course, the wise prepper or survivalist should have both stored food and the capacity to grow and gather additional food for longer emergencies. In this chapter, I will explore the effects of hunger and the power of food on society. All of the great wars, migrations, and revolutions come down to a quest for food. We need oil (energy) so that we can grow, transport, and earn money to get food. Our ancestors migrated, colonized, pioneered, settled, and displaced others for land to produce food. The temporary supply of cheap oil energy and industrialization of farming distracted the masses from the land, but land is the new oil and control of the food supply is (as it always was) the foundation of power.

Most Americans have no concept of what it is like to not have enough food. Our interpretation of being hungry would have been a feast to those who suffered through true famines in Europe and Asia.

As a child I did experience hunger, but I still had some food and enough energy to get to school and play. During the US Civil War and the Great Depression hunger and malnutrition occurred, but not massive starvation. By contrast, Eastern Europe, Africa, and Asia have experienced massive crop failures, wars, and sieges within the past fifty to one hundred years that resulted in significant population reductions and displacements that still affect their societies today. Studying books such as *Leningrad: The Epic Siege of World War II, 1941-1944* (2016) by Anna Reid—who interviewed the survivors of the 872-day siege by German forces that starved approximately 800,000 people to death—gives some indication of what a true famine can do.

As would be expected, the very young and the very old were the first to die off. On a diet that provided from 300 to 800 calories per day, between 5,000 and 10,000 people per month died from July till November. As the cold weather started, death rates rocketed to 55,000 to 110,000 per month until dropping again in June. By then most of the infants, ill, and elderly were gone, along with many others. Not surprisingly, government workers and those with connections fared better. Food crime was rampant. Youths often lurked near the few food-distribution centers and would kill mothers for a few slices of bread or a turnip. Of course, people had no weapons to defend themselves. Early in the siege people would go into the surrounding countryside to trade "valuables" for food from farmers, but soon no amount of gold or jewelry was worth even a bag of potatoes. People with food were hated, even if they were friends or family members. Anyone who looked well fed was under suspicion of hoarding or stealing. People ate boiled leather goods, wallpaper paste, rats, cats, dogs, and tree bark, and even occasionally resorted to cannibalism. All edible game and plant life were gone within the first few months.

Education, wealth, relationships, age, religion—all meant nothing. You had food, or you did not. Food was the common cause. The younger people and those truly committed to the communist state did little to prepare as the German army approached. They had confidence in the state's ability to protect them and to provide for them. This was amplified by the state propaganda that constantly understated the threat. Older people who had experienced famines in the past and those less trusting prepared as best they could. At the beginning of the war, they bought all the bread they could get and dried it in the sun. They even went into the countryside and traded for "cattle cakes" intended to feed cows. They were labeled "alarmist" and "defeatists," so they had to keep a low profile. Does any of this sound familiar?

As the people became weaker and weaker, industry and civil services began to fail, as workers were unable to get to their jobs, much less function. Police, fire, sanitation, and other services were simply unavailable. Even after minimal food supplies were restored, people kept dying. Apparently starvation reaches an irreversible point after which the restoration of food cannot save the life. It appears that after the body consumes its fat, it starts to consume muscle, and then even organ tissue. At this point the body no longer has the capacity to resume digestion and processing of nutrition.

The communist system had completely failed to anticipate or cope with the siege. The population had psychologically abandoned the communist system but had no choice since the enemy at the gate was an even more oppressive force committed to their extermination. Had the enemy been less appalling, the citizens of Leningrad probably would have revolted. When the siege was lifted, the communist government quickly suppressed any reports of the famine and sent many of the most creative survivors to the gulags. Many diaries and photos remained hidden until recently.

CONCLUSION

Hungry people will do anything to get food. They will obey any ruler who can provide food and will attack anyone in order to obtain food. Once food becomes scarce, social relationships, political ideals, religious convictions, and government systems distort, weaken, and fail. Chinese Communist revolutionary Mao Zedong said that "political power grows out of the barrel of a gun," but that is true only if the person holding the gun is well fed. Even in "normal" times, those who control the production and distribution of food have the true economic and political power.

As fuel supplies decline there will be a return to smaller farms and localized supplies. Poor and overpopulated countries will experience increased chaos and death rates. More affluent countries will experience deurbanization, civil unrest, political instability, and shifting values. Major political and economic interests will attempt to retain control of the food supply through regulation, intimidation, and perhaps even rationing. The lucky few who have sufficient food will have a great advantage but will be assaulted both by those who are hungry and those who seek to use food as a source of power and control. Therefore, it is critical that food self-reliance be accompanied by defensive capability. Here are the steps you must take to achieve food freedom:

- Store enough food for short-term (six- to twelve-month) emergencies and to buy time to convert to food self-reliance for longer or indefinite situations.
- Start now to develop food-producing and food-preserving skills and equipment. Hunting, fishing, trapping, and foraging are important, but remember that these resources will quickly be wiped out when everyone is doing them without regulation.
- If you can get a few acres of farmable land, do it now. It will be a good investment (far better than gold) and maybe save your family.
- Start a freedom garden in your yard. Even a small raised-bed, intensive vegetable garden can provide a significant supply of food, but get the experience now. Also start saving vacuum-packed seeds and learn how to create mulch.

- Network with others to build a food trade system in your immediate area. This will necessarily include mutual security for crops, stores, and transport.
- Most important, spread the word and teach the skills of self-reliance. The more people who can take care of their own families, the fewer you have to worry about and the more you can trade with. The more folks who are on your side, the less likely it will be that demigods, gangsters, and dictators will rule the future.

6

Home in the Future

Regardless of how the future "apocalypse" develops, survivors will stay in or return to houses that must be bases for more self-reliant and sustainable living.

INTRODUCTION

Although the term "survival shelter" brings to mind underground bunkers or wilderness lean-tos, for most of us the post-disaster/collapse (whatever it is) shelter will be the place we live in now. If we are forced from our existing home by unpleasant events, we will probably wind up in a house somewhere else. The question we must be ready to answer is: "What will home be like in the new world of the later twenty-first century?"

Home as It Once Was

At the end of the nineteenth century, most homes were essentially self-sufficient. They were built for shelter alone, without utilities and conveniences as we know them today. Lighting (oil lamps), heating (stoves), plumbing (pumps), and sanitation (bed pans or the out-house) were all standalone items. Homes with internal plumbing, gas pipes, sewers, running water, central heating, and indoor toilets only came to be common in the twentieth century. Large vegetable gardens, chicken coops, clotheslines, canning, and other vestiges of self-reliant living remained well into the 1950s. Fireplaces, wood-stoves, and ceiling fans have begun to return to home design as energy costs began their inevitable and unremitting rise. The great majority of today's houses were built after the mid-twenty-first century. These homes are better insulated but often of poorer construction than earlier structures. Their plumbing, heating, and wiring are dependent on fixed and constant voltages, pressures, and sources that may become unreliable in the future. Oversized residences will be expensive or impossible to heat and cool adequately.

Originally a family worked to buy a home that became the base for the whole family as it developed.[3] A bigger place in the same area might be bought by the older members and the smaller place(s) sold (at no interest) to younger family members. Later as they aged, the elderly might go back to the smaller place or a room in the larger abode. Homesteads and stable communities, where everyone knew their neighbors and looked out for each other, were the norm.

In the later twentieth-century, houses came to be thought of as an investment and stopping place rather than a "home." A family would get a "starter home," move to a bigger place to raise kids, and then to a smaller place again at retirement. A house must be thought of as a

---

3   In the early to mid-twentieth century, the average "middle class" family could finance a home and pay it off on one income in about twenty years. Today we have two-income families working for thirty to forty years and still not paying off the mortgage. We no longer have "neighborhoods"; we have "projects" and "developments." The real-estate industry, banks, and taxing agencies want people to keep moving and stay in debt. There is no profit in stable, self-reliant, and secure communities.

base where many of life's needs are met and around which the family works, learns, defends, and grows.

Home as It Will Be

Most modern homes have good insulation and double-paned, tinted windows. If not, these are modern upgrades that everyone should have. If the house does not have a covered front and/or back porch, you should consider adding these improvements. Better yet, have a porch that can be screened and storm windowed. Here is where you can sleep in hot weather, do the laundry in tubs (if necessary), start plants (greenhouse) in early spring, and store firewood. Install rain barrels from your downspouts and consider routing some or all to a basement cistern/tank. Thanks to PVC, this is an easy project. Attached garages can be a benefit, but they also are a liability for fire and other hazards. A detached garage is preferable, but a garage of some kind is a must to shelter vehicles and to store critical supplies.

The backyard should contain a well-organized vegetable garden and maybe fruit trees. Adding a greenhouse or a shed will be a good investment as well. Consider smaller livestock, such as rabbits or chickens, in the future if you have room. At some point you may even need to raise vegetables in the front yard. A high fence will be a big advantage for privacy and security as society changes. Be sure these changes are permitted by local codes and get it done early in your transition plan.

The basement becomes the "engine room" of the house. Here is where indoor edibles can be grown, foods dried or canned, and household products like soap produced and stored. Laundry is dried here in the winter when it's too cold to dry items in the sun. There may be a shop for your home maintenance or even a home-based business in the basement. Now is the time to get that work started.

Heating and lighting extra space will be expensive and maybe impossible in the future. Plan on closing off the "summer rooms" in the winter and just heating the few necessary rooms. You absolutely must have at least one fireplace or stove and a way to close off the room that it's in to conserve heat. Heavy curtains and real shutters will make a comeback.

Electricity will probably continue to be available, but it may be much more costly and force you to limit the use of air conditioners and power tools. It may also be less reliable and prone to brownouts and blackouts. Auxiliary power sources, such as solar panels and wind turbines, will be a good investment over the long term. Be aware that solar, wind, and deep-cycle batteries and even hydrogen are dependent on petroleum products and rare metals that will be depleted by the end of the century. No viable alternative to these alternatives has yet been found. Alternative, nonelectric methods for heat, transportation, light, and other utilities should be considered.

CONCLUSION

Today's houses are poorly constructed to serve as family bases for self-reliant living, but they can be adjusted and retrofitted to provide the necessary facilities and spaces to accommodate a less dependent life-maintenance program. The would-be surviving and thriving family is well advised to acquire a solid house with as much yard space as possible immediately. Do not consider resale value as a primary issue. Consider survivability and adaptability as a home base for life. While the future home will not be like the log cabin, pioneer home of past centuries, it will need to incorporate new adaptations of basic self-sufficiency methods combined with modern and future technologies to assure the security and independence of future families.

7

Hot and Cold

Mark Twain once said, "Mathematicians would tell you that a man standing with one foot in a fire and the other in a bucket of ice water is on average comfortable." Most people are "comfortable" between 65 and 75 degrees Fahrenheit. Our bodies can adjust to cooler and warmer temperatures, but below 45 degrees and above 85 degrees we usually need help from clothing and such devices as heaters, fans, and air conditioners. At further extremes, the issue changes from one of comfort to a matter of survival.

STAYING WARM IN THE WINTER AND COOL IN THE SUMMER UNDER EMERGENCY CONDITIONS

Depending on your location, there are at least six months each year where it is either too cold or too warm to survive without some help. The easy availability of fuel and electricity has led to the placement of major populations in areas that would be (will be) untenable without cheap heating or massive power for air conditioning. Places like Phoenix, Arizona and Minneapolis, Minnesota come to mind. It is highly doubtful that any large urban area could survive long without natural gas for heat and electrical power for air conditioning. While individual homes may adapt, high rises and skyscrapers have no alternative means for heating or cooling. In most cases, the windows don't even open and they sure aren't set up for thousands of stoves. However, urban and suburban homesteads could adapt if preparations are in place.

A BRIEF HISTORY OF HEATING AND COOLING

Prior to World War II, homes were built smaller and thus were easier to heat. Larger homes simply closed off unused rooms in the winter and only heated the ones they used. Older (pre-1920) homes still had gas grates or stoves to heat individual rooms. Sweaters were worn in the home and comforters were often used as well. The temperatures were allowed to get down into the fifties at night, so beds had heavy quilts and even tent-like bed curtains to ward off drafts. Country houses still used true shutters to close off windows against north winds. Coal furnaces were the main source of central heating, and these could burn wood and other solid fuels as well. To keep milk, eggs, and other perishables cool, homes often had a cool storage place for them, often a window with a built-in storage shelf. Hot nightly showers didn't happen. You heated the place up one or two nights a week and everyone took a bath.

To keep cool in summer, windows were double hung so you could open the top and bottom to create circulation. Screen porches provided a safe, insect-free location to catch a breeze. Most folks had beds on these porches so as to sleep in them in the summer. Electric fans provided some comfort, as did cold drinks. Before refrigeration, ice was purchased by the block. This was ice cut from local rivers and lakes and stored in insulated icehouses. Hay was often used to insulate the ice. Ice cut in winter would often last into August if properly stored. Hard physical jobs were performed in the early morning and the late afternoon, not in the middle of the day. Most important, the body adapted to the heat.

After World War II, homes were built bigger and with large rooms that were more costly to heat. Fireplaces were not included in most designs. Smoky coal furnaces were replaced by oil and then natural gas. These were cleaner and better, but less adaptable. In many cases windows no longer opened for ventilation and screen porches disappeared. More recently, better insulation, double-paned windows, and the return of the fireplace have provided some potential for heat conservation.

The point is that we got along without as much heating and almost no air conditioning until the mid-twentieth century. With some adaptation and less comfort, we can again. By the way, I suffered through several winters as a child by collecting coal along the railroad track and scrap wood on my sled to heat our home when we couldn't afford coal. I also lived in an apartment with a fifteen-amp power supply that could scarcely power window fans so I got along for over forty years with no air conditioning at all.

HEATING WITHOUT FUEL OR ELECTRICITY

For short-term interruptions, portable room heaters and blankets may be adequate. Be sure that heaters are designed for indoor use and your carbon monoxide detectors are working. Having a generator that is sufficient (usually 2,000 watts or bigger) to run your furnace fan and controls will be a big help if you still have natural gas supplied. A stove is more efficient than a fireplace. Invest in a wood-burning stove that can quickly be hooked up to the existing fireplace flue. If you have a heat-circulating fireplace, you need to be able to run the fan on alternative power or have an auxiliary fan to move air through the surrounding duct. A small fan that runs on solar rechargeable batteries can effectively move heat from this kind of fireplace to heat a large space.

Camp heaters can be used effectively while the supply of LP gas lasts. A Coleman 3,000 BTU heater will run seven hours on one 16-ounce propane cylinder. That's enough to heat a tent or small room for part of each day. Install doors or set up curtains to close off rooms that do not need to be heated. Seal windows with plastic. Obviously, you are going to need good sleeping bags and wool blankets to conserve your own heat and available fuel. The heat sources will be turned down or off while you're in your sleeping bags or under heavy comforters to conserve fuel. Even so, you will need to have lots of LP gas cylinders or wood to heat and cook with through the worst of the winter.

You may want to consider putting up a small sleeping tent in one room. This will be much easier to heat and will help you retain body heat on cold nights, just like the old bed curtains did. As long as you stay well fed, well clothed, and active, winters will be "cozy" or at least survivable.

STAYING COOL WITHOUT AIR CONDITIONING

In the short term, a generator running a fan or two will be great. You can just find a shady spot and catch a breeze and wait for the power to return. You can usually run your freezer and refrigerator intermittently to save food and provide some ice. You don't have a generator? If the fuel runs out and the power is not going to come back on, you have a few more options. If you cannot build a screen porch, get a screen house that is for campers. You can stay cooler in there and sleep in it at night. You can dig a hole in the yard and line it with hay or build a well-insulated shed to store ice you manufacture in winter by freezing water in containers. Beyond that, you will just have to adapt. Heat will not kill you unless you help it, whereas cold will kill you unless you fight it.

CONCLUSION

We have become accustomed to being perpetually comfortable regardless of the climate, but this may not be the case in the near future. A look at how people in the recent past kept warm and cool offers some hints as to how we may need to adapt in the future. Acquiring the necessary equipment to alter our homes and lifestyles now will be essential to survival in future situations. The combination of climate changes and the diminution of fuel supplies over the next few decades makes the need for adaptation and alternatives to current methods of heating and cooling highly probable.

Note: Camping in all weather conditions is the very best way to assure your ability to survive cold and heat. You will be required to purchase and test stoves, heaters, sleeping bags, clothing, and other necessities. Most important, you will become proficient and confident in your ability to adapt without modern conveniences. Many survival/preparedness groups conduct such activities for this purpose.

8

Cooking When the Gas Goes Off

The ability to cook food, along with the parallel needs to smoke and dry foods and boil water, is an essential survival need. Short-term situations can easily be met with the use of various camping stoves. Long-term loss of natural gas and/or electricity would be a much greater challenge. Even a significant increase in fuel cost or rationing would necessitate the use of alternative methods. The fuel sources used for cooking would compete with the needs for heating and transportation.

The survivor would be wise to have devices to utilize all possible sources of fuel, including wood, kerosene, gasoline, charcoal, LP gas, and solar heat. Since everyone else would be using the same resources, it can be anticipated that wood would disappear rapidly. History tells us that a modest population using wood alone for heating and cooking can decimate acres of forest in a few years. In urban areas that were cut off during past wars, the furniture, fences, and outbuildings quickly went into the fires.

A BRIEF HISTORY OF COOKING

Because cooking is one of man's oldest technologies, it offers the most alternatives and variations. Certainly cooking was discovered almost simultaneously with fire. Anthropologists believe that cooking food was essential to improving mental capacity as civilization developed. Cooked foods provide the body with a much greater share of the starches and proteins and 30 percent more energy than raw foods. In fact, humans can starve to death eating only raw foods.[4]

Open-fire cooking was the predominant method for thousands of years. Pots, pans, grills, and ovens were developed, but the fire remained. The fires came inside as fireplaces and then inside of iron stoves in the 1800s. Gas ranges replaced the smoky and messy woodstoves starting in the late 1800s. Electric ranges and then the microwave finally brought nonfire cooking in the mid-twentieth century. Unfortunately, modern fireplaces are not designed to accommodate the grills and pot hangers that our ancestors cooked on. Most homes are not well suited for installation of wood cooking stoves. The grand wood cooking stoves of old are too heavy and costly ($3,000 to $5,000) for many locations. Fortunately, people have stubbornly hung on to campfire and charcoal cooking methods.

ALTERNATIVES AND OPTIONS

Camp stoves are adequate for short-term emergencies and can be placed on the inactive range under the vent hood. Long-term and large-scale cooking brings the hazards of carbon monoxide, smoke, and fire into the home. Therefore, cooking should be done outside. *Open-fire and charcoal cooking should never, ever, be done inside.*

---

4   Jerry Adler, "Why Fire Makes Us Human," *Smithsonian* Magazine, June 2013 (accessed online).

Liquid fuel stoves should be used with good ventilation and never fueled inside. It would be best to establish a cooking shelter near, but not attached to, the house. Fire extinguishers should always be ready and immediately at hand.

In all but the most inclement weather, cook outside with wood, charcoal, and liquid fuel. Save your LP gas for warming food inside. Solar ovens offer many advantages, but are ineffective during cloudy weather and in extreme cold conditions. Try to plan meals to minimize cooking time and conserve heat. Make one-pot meals cooked in Dutch ovens. Making large one-pot boiled dinners and baking breads for multiple meals while the oven is hot can better utilize fuels.

When selecting foods and cooking utensils, consider how they will be used. Most modern cooking pots and utensils are not designed for use on open fires or in rough conditions. Camp cooking equipment and cast iron cookware are recommended.

In the past the kitchen was in a separate building from the house. This was for safety and to keep the excessive heat and smells isolated. It would be a good idea to have some kind of shelter near the outdoor cooking area so you can cook while protected from sun, rain, and snow. Under extreme conditions, you may have to use a variety of fuels. Each fuel has its advantages and disadvantages. One must also consider space and safety issues when storing fuels. Below are the most likely fuel sources.

- Wood. Smoky and dirty but available for the first months of an emergency. Use a fire pit away from the house. Save your other fuels to use after the wood runs out. Beware of fire hazard!
- Charcoal. Much more efficient than wood. A few briquettes can do a lot of cooking and baking. It is great to use with a Dutch oven. The supply will be limited so use sparingly. Never use in an enclosed space!
- Kerosene. A good hot fuel and safer than gasoline but smelly and sooty.

- Gasoline. Probably in short supply and dangerous to use indoors. Consider it a last resort.
- Alcohol. Clean and renewable with multiple uses.
- LP gas. Various compressed gas stoves are highly effective and safe, but refilling will be highly improbable under disaster conditions. Various cylinders are safe to store, so stock up now.
- Solar. The safest and most economical alternative under most conditions. A solar oven is a must-have.

Fuel availability and the length of any shortages are impossible to predict. Having the widest variety of cooking methods and fuel options is the only way to ensure having hot, safe food throughout long-term situations.

COOKING METHODS AND EQUIPMENT

A wide variety of commercial, improvised, and homemade devices are available. Camp stoves, survival stoves, and military surplus devices abound.

CONCLUSIONS

Most stored survival foods and basic storable foods (e.g., wheat, corn, rice) require cooking. The ability to cook foods has health and psychological benefits that are essential to long-term survival and recovery. A hot cup of coffee and a hot meal can strengthen the body and raise morale. Having a variety of methods and stored fuel supplies will ensure that this basic need is fulfilled under the most difficult conditions.

Portable stove made from an ammunition can.

Homemade can stove using heat tabs.

Corn cooking on a fire pit while canned goods are heated in the bucket of boiling water.

Improvised oven: place four charcoal briquettes on aluminum foil, position four cola cans to hold a baking sheet, and put a cardboard box lined with foil over the top to contain the heat and bake the rolls. This worked great outside on a very cold day.

(Left) One version of a "rocket stove." These stoves will burn twigs or use canned fuels (e.g., alcohol). They are very efficient in the use of fuel and heat conservation, but they must be used outside.

(Below) Solar ovens are available in many sizes. There are also plenty of instructions on how to make them.

Dutch oven cooking with charcoal is very effective. Note that there is some charcoal underneath and some on the cover.

High-Tech BioLite wood-burning camp stove. The stove heat generates electricity that runs a fan to aid the burning, recharges its own battery, and generates enough extra power to charge radios, cameras, flashlights, or cell phones. And it still cooks your meal!

9

Medical Care for Yourself

Modern medicine has made great advances in the past few decades. Unfortunately, much of this care is tied to a failing economy and declining resources. Our society has become increasingly dependent on a complex and costly medical care system for even the most minor illnesses and injuries. Additionally, our civilization has created hundreds of new medical problems—real and imaginary. Medical care is a "bubble" that, like the housing bubble, will burst under the stress of environmental and economic disasters. While there will be no replacement for some advanced medical care and medications, individuals, families, and communities can take steps to improve their chances of avoiding, preventing, or surviving medical emergencies when access to advanced professional care is unaffordable or unattainable.

A BRIEF HISTORY OF MEDICAL CARE

Ancient man tried all sorts of potions, ceremonies, and even surgeries with stone tools to cure himself when ill or injured. Some of them even worked. The ancient Greeks formalized medical care and wrote the Hippocratic oath, which among other things required practitioners to promise to "reject harm and mischief," which is commonly interpreted today as "first do no harm." Of course, the various medicine men and doctors through the ages *did* further harm. A few herbal remedies and chemical formulas were actually effective in treating some symptoms, but there were no dramatic improvements in medical care from the time of Christ up until the nineteenth century. Small wounds could lead to death, as could such illnesses as the flu, measles, and diabetes. Child mortality was high, and massive plagues periodically reduced populations by up to 50 percent. Armies usually lost more men to diseases than to combat injuries, and the average life expectancy remained at about forty to fifty years old. In the 1800s advanced surgery, anesthesia, immunization, sterilization, sanitation, and some effective medications came into general use. These advances improved one's chances of survival and lengthened the average life expectancy.

As the twentieth century unfolded, the industrial revolution provided mass-produced surgical equipment and chemical medications. Science developed antibiotics and advanced diagnostic tools such as X-rays. Still, healthcare was generally affordable and personal until it became an "industry" in recent decades. Prior to World War II, most doctors were general practitioners, or "family doctors," who had an office of their own and worked at one or more hospitals. There were surgeons, pediatricians, and a few other specialists, but nothing like today. If you had a minor injury (e.g., burn, cut, sprain) or illness (e.g., flu, cold, upset stomach), you probably didn't even think of calling the doctor. You had plenty of home remedies and family care. If it was a bit worse, you could call the doctor and he would come by your home or you could go to his office. The doctor's office was set up to set broken bones and even some minor surgery. Ambulances and hospitals were the last resort for very serious situations.

The cost of medical insurance was pretty reasonable since it was not used for minor problems and medical costs were not nearly as high (inflation adjusted) as they are today. In fact, the insurance "industry" pushed the medical profession to raise rates to force more people to get medical insurance and eventually allied with them to create a noncompetitive medical industry that put injured and ill consumers at their mercy. Effective lobbying brought governmental support disguised as regulations that created today's massive, complex, and unsustainable health care system. Thanks to governmental interference and warped economics, it is predicted that we will have a shortage of 45,000 primary care physicians and 46,000 surgeons by the year 2020. By the year 2025, there will be a shortage of at least 130,000 physicians to provide care for a growing and aging population. Now consider the problems in an epidemic or other mass casualty situation.

REALITY CHECK: WHAT WILL HAPPEN WHEN THE DOCTOR IS NO LONGER IN?

- A significant part of the population remains alive only because of available medications and care systems. Patients with transplants, pacemakers, heart medications, thyroid medications, diabetes, chronic obstructive pulmonary disease, kidney failure, cancer, and many other conditions will die within weeks or months without advanced care and costly medications. The fact is that any significant disruption of the economy, fuel, transportation, and energy will collapse these highly vulnerable medical care systems almost immediately. Conservatively, 10 percent of the population cannot survive even a two- to four-month interruption of care.

- Many more depend on medications and therapy to prevent the onset of serious and debilitating illness. Those with severe arthritis, high cholesterol, existing infection, and other conditions are likely to develop debilitating and fatal results within months or a few years once deprived of medication.

- Another significant portion of the population depends on preventive and supportive care and therapy to avoid catastrophic illness or just to maintain life-sustaining activities. This group includes the disabled, mentally challenged, and the elderly.

- The decline and possible collapse of the economic infrastructure will undoubtedly reduce the availability of safe food and water. This will lead to an increase in a wide variety of illnesses and epidemics. Much of today's population has weakened immune systems due to the overuse of antibiotics and disinfectants. This combined with a shortage of vaccines and antibiotics will lead to many deaths.

- Last, but not least, people will be forced to engage in activities for which they have no past experience or skills. Poor sanitation, improper food preparation, and the use of tools, generators, stoves, fuels, axes, and firearms will generate a high number of serious injuries and medical conditions that will require advanced care just when it is least available.

The result of all of the above factors will be a 10 to 20 percent death rate in the first one or two years and a rising rate for decades, leveling off to a lower life expectancy for the survivors by the end of the century.

WHAT CAN YOU DO NOW?

- Stock up on any prescription medications and medical supplies that you can get your hands on. These can buy time or even save lives in a medium-term disaster. Most medications are effective far past their expiration dates.

- Medications are only tested for two years to establish the expiration date so they can sell you more meds. Keep them in a cool place, vacuum packed, and away from children. *Only* use them as a last resort. Oxygen (medical grade) is one thing that can truly save lives in some situations. If you can stock a few cylinders with a regulator and some non-rebreather masks, do so.

- Maximize the opportunities to get healthy now. Get every immunization you can. If you smoke, *stop!* Eat healthy and get exercise to maintain heart health. Take care of any medical conditions, such as hernias, while you can. Take care of your teeth; dental problems can lead to other illness later when you can't survive them. You do not want to have unnecessary issues that you can avoid or fix now. All your survival food and equipment will not save you from poor health.

- Build a network of medically skilled friends and associates. Preparedness groups should make this a priority. Yes, having food and other things to trade for medical care will be well worth the effort. Nursing skills may be as important as doctors for long-term care.

- Learning first aid and, if possible, EMT skills is a must. Wound management and extended care for illness will be particularly important. This should be combined with building up a stock of basic care supplies, such as sterile instruments, gauze pads, tape, vinyl gloves, and antiseptics. Don't forget over-the-counter medications and pain relievers.

- Consider studying alternative medications derived from wild plants. While some of these "herbal remedies" are less effective than others, they do offer some relief and comfort when traditional medications are unavailable.

- Become more generally self-reliant. Being able to avoid contact with the population may prevent many contagious illness and violence-related injuries. Experience with treating injuries and illnesses at home now will build skills for the future. Knowing how to use survival equipment now will avoid injuries (e.g., cuts, burns, fractures) later.

- Stock up on basic sanitation supplies, such as bleach, alcohol, soap, mouthwash, insecticides, and peroxide. Keeping clean and free of infection will be critical.

- Build up a library of medical references. This may be all you have to go with in an extreme and long-term situation. See recommendations below.

RECOMMENDED BOOKS

There are literally hundreds of basic first-aid books that cover primary wound care, splinting, cardiopulmonary resuscitation, and management of illnesses in expectation of available medical support. I recommend that the reader buy ones that are sold at outdoor sports stores. These usually assume that you will be on your own for a while and may need to improvise. The four books below go well beyond basic care.

- *Special Operations Forces Medical Handbook,* US Department of Defense, Skyhorse Publishing. Covers advanced medical techniques, including sanitation, obstetrics, dentistry, veterinary medicine, and wound management.
- *Emergency War Surgery,* US Department of the Army, Skyhorse Publishing. Covers advanced orthopedics, wound management, and infection control.
- *The Merck Manual,* Merck Inc., home edition by Pocket Books of London. A very thorough (1,700-plus-page) reference on diagnosis, care, and medications.

- *Ditch Medicine,* by High L. Coffee from Paladin Press. A well-illustrated manual on advanced care of trauma injuries.

You may also want to get the latest edition of *Emergency Care and Transportation of the Sick and Injured* published by the American Academy of Orthopedic Surgeons. This is the standard manual for EMTs and covers a wide variety of injuries and illnesses in a very organized way.

MEDICINAL PLANTS AND HERBS

The effectiveness of medicinal plants is well documented, and while more modern medications have surpassed most of them in safety and effectiveness, they may offer the only alternative under future conditions. *The Herbalist* by Joseph E. Meyer was first published in 1918, and many modern versions of this book can be found today. These books include a cross index of medicinal plants and what they are used to treat. They include details on what part of the plant to use, how to prepare the medication, and how to use it. Most also include illustrations or photographs of the plant and information on where they can be found. You will want to have at least one *Herbalist* book in your library.

A few good examples of common medicinal plants are chamomile, catnip, mint, thyme, feverfew, sage, plantain, willow bark, lungwort, horehound, and boneset.

Examples of Herbal Remedies and Plants

Treatment for Colds

One teaspoon each of yarrow, boneset, mint, catnip, verbena, and horehound plus 1/2 teaspoon of sage. Mix one teaspoon of the above in one cup of hot water and steep covered for ten minutes. Drink a cup every two to three hours.

Comfrey: used often as a decongestant. Wikipedia: Finchj.

Chamomile: often used as a mild sedative and for stomach cramps. Wikipedia/Kallerna.

Boneset: Used as a diaphoretic and emetic. Wikipedia/I, SB Johnny.

Treatment for Influenza

One teaspoon each of cinnamon, sage, and bay leaf. Mix 1 teaspoon of the above in one cup of hot water and steep covered for ten minutes. Drink a cup freely.

A Few Improvised Medical Techniques and Formulas

Pain Relief

The combination of two acetaminophen and three ibuprofen tablets taken together is safe and will give pain relief comparable to codeine.

Dakin's Solution

Dakin's solution can be used to soak dressings for shallow wounds and flush deep wounds while healing. It was used to reduce gangrene during World Wars I and II before penicillin was available.

- Boil four cups of clean water for fifteen minutes.
- Add 1/2 teaspoon of baking soda and let cool.
- Add three ounces of bleach.
- Store in sealed container protected from light.

Saline (Salt) Solution

Saline solution can be used to flush wounds and maintain bandage moisture.

Make a 100 percent saline solution by adding salt slowly to warm water and mixing. When the salt starts to settle to the bottom instead of mixing, it is 100 percent saturated. Pour off the solution without the settled crystals. You can now mix this with sterile water to make 50 percent, 20 percent, or any other percentage solution you desire. "Normal" saline is 9 percent.

Rehydration Solution

Dehydration is one of the primary causes of death, secondary to shock, heat stroke, radiation sickness, and many communicable diseases. If ambulance and emergency room treatment is not immediately available and the patient is fully conscious, oral hydration can be sustained using the following solution:

Eight teaspoons of sugar and one teaspoon of salt to one liter of water. Provide small four-ounce drinks every hour.

Caution: Giving water or other liquids to an unconscious, semi-conscious, or seriously injured patient may cause vomiting and aspiration, which can result in pneumonia. Generally, these patients can be rehydrated by intravenous methods at the emergency room.

Water Purification

Mix eight to sixteen drops of bleach per gallon of water.

Decontamination Solution

This is a 10 percent bleach-water solution. You can use it as a spray or wash.

Super Glue

Super Glue can be used to close shallow wounds, but not deep wounds.

Saran Wrap

Saran Wrap can be used to bandage large wounds and hold dressings and splints in place.

MENTAL HEALTH AND MEDICAL CARE

Government regulation of medical care has inevitably led to growing abuse of freedom. Access to care will increasingly involve intrusion and oppression of personal liberties. Questions such as, "Do you own a gun?" or "Have you ever been arrested?" will lead to further questions about your organizational involvements and past activities. Any number of factors can be used to determine your "mental health." Critical health care may be denied to those unwilling to answer questions or cooperate. People may be denied health care for noncompliance and denied freedoms (e.g., gun ownership, travel) if they do. This is basically a pacification and extermination program for individualists and independent thinkers. This may be the best reason of all to develop alternative medical care networks.

CONCLUSION

It is difficult to predict exactly how or when the medical care system will disintegrate. It continues to grow bigger and more costly even as the economic and practical viability weakens. Epidemics will become more frequent. Disasters that overwhelm the system will erode confidence. The availability of care and medications will become more and more unreliable and ineffective. It is more likely to degenerate in stages than to collapse all at once. No doubt, a combination of family self-help, community-based home care, and more empowered local medical services will emerge. Of course, there will also be black-market medicine and scam medical services. Educated and networked families will have access to effective and compassionate medical aid for many types of illnesses and injuries, but many will not be able to find treatment of advanced and complex illnesses for some time, depending on the situation.

10
Personal Hygiene

We take the ability to stay clean for granted, but it may become more difficult to do so in the future. Fortunately, there are practical alternatives to our current methods of personal hygiene.

INTRODUCTION AND HISTORY

Americans are arguably the cleanest people on Earth. Having been blessed with a plentiful supply of clean water early in our history and the Christian "cleanliness is next to godliness" ethos, we regard frequent bathing, toothbrushing, and general hygiene as standards of civilized living. In ancient times, private bathing was reserved for the wealthy, who could afford a costly bathtub and servants to fill it. The remainder of the population had to bathe in the rivers or public baths. The use of rivers and public baths are still common in third world countries. In cold climates and where water was at a premium, bathing might be limited to a few times per year. Guess why perfume and incense were invented! Often, the same soap was used to wash faces, take baths, wash hair, and lather up to shave with. Running water and water heaters were not universal until the mid-twentieth century, so public baths and semiprivate baths that you could take at a barbershop were still common. I still remember the bathtub in a stall at the Hotel Florence barbershop in Chicago in the 1960s. Shaving was accomplished using a shaving brush and mug to create lather and a straight razor. Witch hazel was the general-purpose aftershave that worked well. Canned shaving cream and disposable razors are a fairly recent innovation.

Showers often replaced the bath in today's fast-paced society and are actually more efficient and use less water. Temporary or permanent shortages of water and the energy to heat it may necessitate a return to more conservative bathing methods and schedules. This does not mean that we cannot maintain high standards of personal hygiene.

Toothbrushing became common in the United States about the time of the American Revolution. Poor dental hygiene is still common in most of the world. Our high-sugar and high-acid diets have made brushing and flossing essential.

ALTERNATIVES AND IMPROVISATIONS

We use far more water, soap, and other personal cleaning supplies than are necessary. The market sells us on using all sorts of soaps, shampoos, conditioners, deodorants, moisturizers, creams, and bath aids that waste our money, pollute our water, and often do more harm than good to us. A practical return to more conservative methods can save money and may be necessary in the future. There were periods in my life where abundant hot water was not available. The house was cold in winter for lack of fuel, and a fast "sponge bath" was the best one could do. A thorough sponge bath taken with a warm, soapy sponge or washcloth and then a rinsing wet towel can be as effective as a fast shower. Be sure to cover the floor with towels to avoid slipping. Soapy towels and washcloths can become breeding grounds for mildew and mold; they must be rinsed and dried effectively before reuse.

Assuming that the bathtub's drain still works, there are several ways to improvise showers. Sun Showers and other hanging-bag-type shower devices designed for camping can be used indoors if necessary. Keep in mind that these are pretty heavy when filled with water and you may need to establish a strong anchor point on the ceiling above your tub from which to hang them. Of course, in warm weather they can be used outdoors in an enclosed stall or while you are wearing a bathing suit. Another alternative is to use a garden sprayer tank. Pumped up with pressure, one of these can provide a good shower with a small volume of water. With a little work, it can be modified to self-administer the shower, or you can have a family member do it. These are the same devices commonly used for chemical and biological decontamination.

In between sponge baths and improvised showers, you must wash your face, feet, underarms, and genital area at least daily. Daily toothbrushing and flossing are also essential. Dental problems when there is no dentist available can be a serious survival issue, and bad teeth often lead to other ailments.

You may notice that there were a lot more beards in the "old days." That's because it was easier to trim a beard with a knife or scissors than shave daily in the backwoods. That may return, but most men will prefer daily shaving. Any bar soap remnants can be placed in a mug and brushed into a lather with a shaving brush. Currently available disposable razors can be stretched to last for up to a month; but when the supply runs out, you will need to have a straight-razor that can be sharpened indefinitely. Shaving with one of these takes more care and, yes, you will get cut a few times until you get the hang of it. Ouch!

Badger fur shaving brushes can still be purchased for $20 to $50, but a good one can last a lifetime. Straight razors are still available but expensive at $75 to $120. A full kit with the razor, razor strap, and sharpening stone runs about $180 but lasts almost forever. You may get lucky at a garage sale and get used stuff for next to nothing. Soap mugs with soap run about $20 each, but you can improvise. The alternative is to stock up on disposable razors or old double-edged razors and blades now. Witch hazel is a great astringent aftershave that is also useful for rashes, itches, acne, bruises, and hair care. You can get it for less than $5 per quart at most pharmacies. Since witch hazel is a natural derivative of an herbal shrub, you could make your own in the future.

Homemade Toothpaste

You can make toothpaste at home with the following ingredients and formulas:

Formula #1

- 2/3 cup baking soda
- 4 teaspoons sea salt
- 2 teaspoons peppermint oil
- Mix to a paste and keep covered.

Formula #2

- 6 pints baking soda
- 1 pint vegetable-based glycerin
- 1 pint hydrogen peroxide
- Mix to a paste and keep covered.

Homemade Soap

The most important element of cleanliness is soap. Knowing how to make your own soap for personal use and trade is a valuable skill. There are many kinds of kits and methods for making soap, but I prefer the "pioneer" method because it uses lye that can be made from ashes and fat that can be rendered from cooking—two ingredients that are available regardless of economic conditions. Some people add herbs or oils (e.g., rose, lilac, mint) to the soap.

Required Materials

- Clean animal fat
- Lye
- Water

Required Equipment

- Clear 2-quart plastic bottle (such as juice bottle)
- Rubber gloves, apron, and eye protection
- Wooden mixing spoon or stick
- Large 10–12-quart pot *(never* use aluminum with lye)
- Candy or dairy thermometer
- Heavy cardboard or wooden box lined with plastic or greased with petroleum jelly (for molding soap)
- Insulation (such as cardboard, foam, or blanket material)
- Newspapers to protect working surfaces and floor

Instructions

- Prepare the lye solution by slowly adding and mixing 13 ounces of lye to 2 1/2 pints of cold water.
- Caution: Never add water to lye. This solution will self-heat to about 200°F.
- Let this solution cool to about 98°F.
- Heat 6 pounds of fat to about 98°F in a tub of hot water— *never* over a flame.
- Slowly pour the warm lye solution into the warm fat and stir until you have an opaque, creamy solution.
- Pour the solution into a mold about 1 to 1 1/2 inches thick.
- Cover with insulation to ensure slow cooling.
- When the solution is cooled and solidified, cut it into bars.

Making Lye for Soap Production

Fill a barrel or other nonmetallic container with wood ashes. Place a layer of straw at the bottom of the barrel to filter the liquid precipitate, and a hole at the bottom or low on the side to let the lye drip out. Then add boiling water slowly to the top and let it seep down through the ash until it starts to drip from the hole into a plastic or glass container (see drawing on next page). Test the lye by cracking a raw egg into it. If it barely floats, the lye is usable to make soap.

Caution: Lye is a very corrosive material. It will damage eyes and burn skin quickly. It is also particularly reactive with aluminum. Wear rubber gloves, rubber aprons, and goggles and have water to

flush off splashes immediately and repeatedly. Use glass and plastic containers.

THINGS TO STOCK UP ON

Not everything will be easy to replace. The following items are cheap today and would be well worth stocking up on for future shortages.

- Toothbrushes and toothpaste
- Dental floss
- Razors
- Soap
- Mouthwash
- Witch hazel
- Shampoo
- Talcum powder
- Nail clippers
- Washcloths
- Baking powder

CONCLUSION

Your health and morale depend on personal cleanliness. While adjustments may be necessary under future conditions, there is no excuse for reverting to being dirty and unhygienic. By establishing regular cleaning habits using more efficient and practical methods, everyone can continue to be clean and neat through future situations. Stocking up on basic supplies and a few essential pieces of equipment is key to a successful transition.

11

Human Waste Sanitation Alternatives

Sanitation is the most often ignored subject of survival and self-reliance preparation. At best it is touched on in short-term preparedness manuals and military manuals. These publications assume that normal sewage systems will be functional for a short time or that (in the case of the military) the site will be moved in a few days or weeks. The challenges of an indefinite or permanent loss of sanitation systems in a highly populated area are seldom addressed. In this chapter we will cover the needs of immediate sanitation for the short term (a few days to seven weeks), as well as coping with the permanent termination of sewage systems.

A BRIEF HISTORY OF SEWERS

Once humans began to permanently inhabit large towns the accumulation and disposal of human waste became a problem. In fact, the ability to cope with human waste was the key to the rise of the city-states and of advanced civilizations. Most ancient cities were built on rivers and near the ocean to provide a convenient method of flushing away waste. While Rome and many other cities did have some fairly sophisticated underground sewers, they served only a small part of the population. Open sewers, gutters, and "honey wagons" that carried human waste to the nearest waterway, and outhouses served the peripheral areas.

Sewage limited the growth of cities to thousands or a few hundred thousand through the eighteenth century. In town, outhouses were common right up to the early twentieth century. A city could grow only as far as the technology for waste disposal would permit. When this was exceeded, disease usually reduced the population quickly. Only the advent of steam- and diesel-powered digging equipment in the late nineteenth and early twentieth centuries permitted the construction of massive piped sewage systems that made it possible for millions to live in crowded cities without being buried in waste or cut down by diseases. Until the mid-twentieth century, most systems depended on gravity to sustain a flow to the outlet, but as cities grew it was necessary to pump sewerage and treat it before discharge. Most sewage systems today are dependent on constant maintenance and power.

WHAT COULD HAPPEN

Any kind of lengthy interruption of power, fuel, or chemical supplies would cause a shutdown of sewage systems. Civil disorder, epidemics, or economic collapse would certainly mean the abandonment of these complex facilities. Even general budget cuts could eventually result in system failures and unrepaired collapses. Keep in mind that any failures of the sanitation system will immediately impact the safety of the water supply and result in spreading diseases. While the toilets may be flushed for a while, the sewage will eventually fill the sewers and back up into streets and homes in the lowest areas first. Untreated sewage may also flow into the rivers and lakes. Urban areas will become stinking, fly-infested, and disease-ridden hells.

Any citizens dependent on the existing water supplies or sanitation systems will be forced to abandon their homes or die. As with water, food, and fuel, big cities are untenable without existing technological systems.

Short-Term Sanitation

In short-term emergencies, the sewage system may still be functional for weeks. Although the water to flush the existing toilets may be hard to spare, so-called "brown water" from bathing and cleaning can be used to flush the toilet. Dumping about a gallon of any kind of water will cause it to flush. Rainwater, pond water, or water from another source can be used for this purpose.

If the toilet is not available at all, you can improvise one using a five-gallon pail lined with a heavy-duty plastic bag. As it fills, add some bleach and bury it in the backyard if possible. This is one of the reasons to have bleach, plastic bags, buckets, and shovels. Waste can also be dumped into a pit with quick lime and covered. In Vietnam, American servicemen often burned human waste in oil drums using gasoline. While effective, it is unlikely you will have fuel to waste, and no one will appreciate the smell.

Basic Porta Potty kit consisting of a toilet seat mounted on a bag-lined five-gallon pail. It sells for about $28, or you can make your own for less.

Long-Term Sanitation Facilities

Small towns with gravity-operated systems and uphill well-water supplies may do okay

Basic shallow-pit toilets. Note the shovel to cover the waste with dirt and the handy toilet paper holder. Such facilities would be sufficient for the short term or in temporary camps only.

during a catastrophe. Most suburban and urban areas will experience traumatic population reductions through epidemics, famine, evacuation, and violence. The shortages of water, food, and other critical needs will probably thin the population before the sanitation systems fail completely.

Outhouses

Those having access to large lots can probably build outhouses. These "facilities" provide a reasonably safe and sanitary means of waste disposal. Screening and proper ventilation will keep flies out and prevent the accumulation of flammable gases. Yes, they can blow up! My grandfather had a permanent outhouse about 200 feet from the house. He had a small toilet room inside for use at night and in cold weather. Someone had to haul the bucket out and dump it in the outhouse hole every morning—lots of fun. There was a bucket of "quick lime" and a scoop in the outhouse. So after the contents had been dumped, a scoop of lime was tossed in to start breaking down

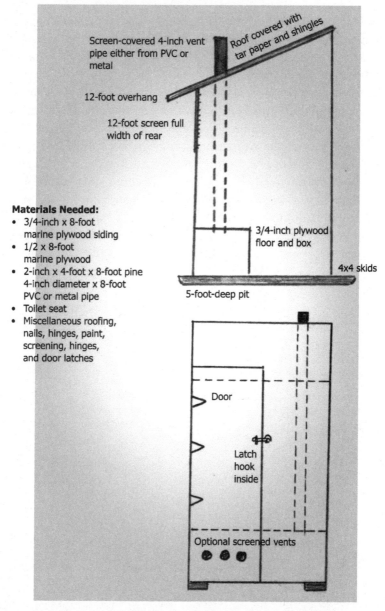

Screen-covered 4-inch vent
pipe either from PVC or
metal

Roof covered with
tar paper and shingles

12-foot overhang

12-foot screen full
width of rear

3/4-inch plywood
floor and box

4x4 skids

5-foot-deep pit

Materials Needed:
- 3/4-inch x 8-foot
  marine plywood siding
- 1/2 x 8-foot
  marine plywood
- 2-inch x 4-foot x 8-foot pine
  4-inch diameter x 8-foot
  PVC or metal pipe
- Toilet seat
- Miscellaneous roofing,
  nails, hinges, paint,
  screening, hinges,
  and door latches

Door

Latch
hook
inside

Optional screened vents

The building is 4x4x8 feet high in front and six-feet high at the rear, with a two-feet-wide by 6.5-inch-high door.

the waste. If you don't have quick lime, you can use ashes from your fireplace instead. My grandfather also had a movable outhouse. He planted pumpkins on the old location and got a 70-pound pumpkin that won the county fair!

Depending on your location and the materials available, you may choose to build a permanent facility or a movable one. If you choose to have a permanent location you will need to have a large hatch in the lower rear of the structure to remove the accumulated waste. You can either have a bucket in there that needs to be emptied every few days into a remotely located pit or a lined box that you rake out and shovel every week or so. More fun. If you have enough room to move the outhouse around, you will need to build it on skids so it can be towed from place to place. It will need to be moved every time the pit gets about half full. That means digging a pit and then

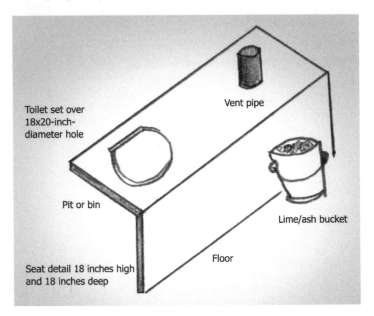

If a pit is used, it should be four-feet wide by four-feet wide by about five-feet deep. Move the building when the hole is half full. Any waste disposal pit should be at least 300 feet from your water source.

covering it. You can build an outhouse from plywood or convert a prefabricated shed into one.

This assumes that municipal regulations are no longer an issue under these conditions. The illustration on the following page is based on one that Live Free members built in the 1980s. This design met international standards for size and ventilation. Shortages of materials may force you to make some compromises and adaptations.

Note: Painting all surfaces will help prevent rotting. Be sure to bend or cut off any protruding nail as even a scratch can cause infection.

CONCLUSION

Any disruption of the sanitation system will cause massive problems and epidemics. The true survivor must be prepared to cope with the short- and medium-term issues of human waste disposal. If there is a complete and sustained breakdown of urban and suburban sewage systems, areas with high population density will become untenable. Suburbs and smaller towns may be able to sustain occupancy and recover if they are able to effectively adapt to sanitation methods that have worked in the past. Would-be survivors should have all the necessary items for short-term sanitation and at least the basic materials and knowledge to go further if necessary.

12

What to Do with the Garbage

Like flushing the toilet, disposing of garbage is one of those things that we do not want to think about. But the day that the garbage trucks stop showing up, we *will* think about it a lot! Recent emergencies and strikes have demonstrated that even a short interruption in this service can bring an urban economy to a halt and generate a serious health hazard. A long-term interruption of just this one service would turn towns and cities into an untenable nightmare. As budgets tighten and municipal governments start to fail, garbage collection will become increasingly expensive and unreliable. In a severe disaster, it may be interrupted or even suspended indefinitely. Having a plan and the necessary equipment to dispose of your own waste will be essential to the health of your family and your community.

A BRIEF HISTORY OF GARBAGE

In the distant past, garbage and human waste were just dumped or, at best, buried around the camp. Once the area was thoroughly polluted, the tribe moved on. Cities and towns generally burned trash right near the population centers. The term "bonfire" was originally "bone fire" because the garbage and waste that were burned contained bones. Prior to the 1940s, the volume of trash and garbage generated by the average urban household was far less than it is today. Trash cans were usually small, galvanized twenty- to thirty-gallon containers. The contents were periodically emptied into dump trucks and hauled to the "city dump." A lot of nice suburban houses now sit on those dump sites. Garbage consisted of mostly food waste and some empty cans and bottles. Kids did paper drives and collected most of the excess newspapers. Kids also gathered bottles and took them in for the deposit money. Since most people had coal-burning furnaces or fireplaces, a lot of the waste paper and cardboard was used for heat. Lots of folks mulched for their gardens and did canning with reusable jars.

Right after World War II, the volume of garbage and trash generated per household exploded along with the population. The rise of the supermarket and the two-job family brought a huge increase in prepackaged foods wrapped in cardboard, plastic, and paper. With Mom working, there was much less cooking from scratch with fresh ingredients, and lots more cans and boxes were used.

"Repairable" was replaced by "disposable," which added packaging and all sorts of junk to the pile. Then came disposable diapers and cat litter. The first attempt to cope with this wave of garbage was to mandate the installation of concrete "incinerators" behind each home. These contraptions had a hatch at the top for dumping your garbage and a hatch facing the alley for the city trash collectors to shovel out the ashes and scorched remnants. What? That's right, you were expected (by law) to burn your garbage on a specified day. The aroma on that day was quite invigorating. Eventually, the cities constructed huge incinerator plants with very tall chimneys, and garbage was emptied from the fifty-five-gallon drum in your alley into the purpose-built garbage trucks we know today. When the air pollution from the city incinerators became a problem, landfills were created. These abominations destroyed a great deal of the wetlands and drainage systems around our towns and cities. Only modest progress in waste reduction and recycling has been achieved since then, while the population and waste generation continues to grow. Our society and economies continue to drown in our own waste. This wastefulness has contributed to the inevitable failure of the culture that created it.

The good news (if you can call it that) is that economic decline and disaster will inevitably reduce the volume of waste per family. Unfortunately, it may also reduce the number of people creating any kind of waste. At any rate, we do not need to plan on how to dispose of the current three to five cubic feet of garbage and trash per person per week that we generate now, but just the one or two that we would generate in a post disaster, self-reliant, efficient economy. Let's look at each category of waste (other than sanitary waste) as it could be managed in an urban or suburban environment. Those living in rural areas will probably still be able to burn or bury waste well away from their homes.

TRUE GARBAGE

True garbage is waste food, spoiled meat, rotting vegetables, coffee grounds, and various materials contaminated with blood and juices. This is the stuff that is going to attract rodents, insects, and disease to you and your community. It cannot be permitted to accumulate. A combination of all four methods below will be needed.

- Minimize the generation of these wastes by careful meal planning and effective use (consumption) of all possible foods. Remember that you may not have refrigeration or a microwave. When excess is available, dry, can, cure, and smoke meats, fruits, and vegetables. Make effective use of vegetables as soup and stews.
- Mulch vegetable wastes, garden wastes, grass clippings, etc. You will need this to fertilize your garden. No more "Shake and Grow" from the store. Get started with mulching now so you have the equipment and experience.

- Burn meat wastes and other biologically hazardous wastes. Purchase a screen-covered fire pit, or prepare a thirty- or fifty-five-gallon drum for this purpose by placing holes around the lower third of the drum. Another option is to make an enclosure out of heavy expanded metal to burn waste outside without scattering ashes and embers.
- Bury ashes and anything you can't burn. This should be a fairly small amount. If you can find a place away from your home to bury this kind of safe material, do so.

PAPER AND CARDBOARD

In the reduced economy, there should be a 75 to 90 percent reduction in this kind of waste. No newspapers or junk mail coming to your door, and no boxes from packaged foods and unnecessary appliances. A fireplace or stove should turn this stuff into heat. An outdoor fire pit is another less efficient option.

GLASS

There will be a drastic reduction in this material also, but not as much as paper and plastic. Fortunately, there are a lot of uses for glass containers. Craft shops offer some kits for converting bottles into glassware. Start canning and build up a stock of the reusable jars, caps, and seals.

METAL CANS

Again, there will be a lot fewer of these to worry about. Many so-called survival foods do come in cans, so this may generate a lot of cans while you are using up that stuff. One use for empty cans is as starter pots for plants. Steel cans will rust away pretty fast after burning off the coatings. Aluminum cans are very thin and can be flattened to take up very little room. There may or may not be a market for them in the future economy.

PLASTIC

Fortunately, plastic will almost go away in a declining economy. Plastic items you have (e.g., buckets, coolers, containers) should last indefinitely. Unfortunately, some of it will be waste and will be indestructible. Burning is messy, toxic, and ineffective. If you cannot think of a use for it, crush, bundle, and bury.

CONCLUSION

If all this seems like a lot of work, remember that at least one family member (maybe both) will not have a job and everyone needs more exercise. A changing "lifestyle" is not going to be a choice unless you want to be one of those people shown on TV with a house and yard filled with garbage and trash. This is just one of the many challenges that must be solved by the truly free and self-reliant family.

13

Laundry

Having clean clothes is taken for granted. Doing laundry has become easy with modern automatic washers and dryers. The potential interruption of electrical power and natural gas supplies, or just the rising cost of these steadily dwindling resources, may make it necessary to revert to earlier methods. Fortunately, with a little extra equipment, hand laundering can be achieved. All you need is a little elbow grease.

A BRIEF HISTORY OF LAUNDRY DAY

Like cooking, clothing repairing, and food preservation, doing laundry was once a real chore. "Laundry day" meant exactly that. Before the turn of the century, laundry was done by hand. In any weather above freezing, it was done outside on the back porch in a large "washtub." After washing and then hand-wringing or using a cranked wringer, the pieces were hung up on clotheslines to dry. This added up to a lot of dumping of soapy water, splashing water, and dripping clothes, and thus was a process much better done outside the house. In winter, laundry could be done in the basement if it had a paved floor or just put off till spring. Clothing was worn until it was dirty, not changed daily.

The powered agitator washing machine with its wringer device came into general use in the early 1920s and continued into the early 1950s. You still needed to hang clothing out to dry or dry it on lines in the basement. Basement drying helped keep up the humidity in the house, but the clothing usually smelled like coal or oil from the heating system. The modern washer and dryer liberated the basement and the housewife from "laundry day."

Laundry is still a bit of a task but not nearly as odious as it once was. I find it interesting that all the talk about "going green" and energy conservation never suggests going back to outdoor clothes drying . . . must be the home appliance lobby at work there.

Double washtubs with hand wringer and washboard (far right) all in a sturdy stand. This may be a replacement for washing machines in future situations.

BASIC LAUNDRY TOOLS

Washtubs

These are two-foot (and larger) diameter, twelve- to twenty-four-inch deep galvanized steel tubs with handles. They come in many sizes from eight to thirty-five gallons. Granger, Harbor Freight, and many other suppliers still have these at about $35 each. You will need to have two or three of these, one for washing and one or two for rinsing. They are heavy when filled and will need to be pumped or bailed out, so put them on a strong stand or table, with the top of the tub about waist high. Under survival conditions you may need to

Alternative method: Amish clothes boiler. Boiling ensured clean clothing without needing to use soap. This method uses a lot more fuel than just heating water a bit to wash with soap. This farmhouse had a side-room devoted to clothes washing and drying.

use these to gather rainwater when not in use. You may also need to use the used laundry and rinse water for other purposes.

Hand Washing Devices

These are replacements for the agitator, and they look like common plungers. In fact, you can use a plunger if nothing else is available. You just plunge the clothing in the soap water to force the dirt out. No rocket science here. You will want to go easy on the soap because (1) its valuable and (2) you need to rinse it out with the minimum of water. If you can hang it out on a rainy day, nature will rinse it for you, but you will have to wait for a sunny day to get it dry. But it will be clean and smell good!

Scrubbing Boards

Washboards are made of corrugated tempered glass or galvanized metal. They provide a smooth but wavy surface against which you can scrub tough dirt out of clothing. This is a must-have, but it can be rough on clothing and should be used sparingly. A scrub board costs about $30 today. A good soft-bristled brush is handy for those dirty spots too.

Wringers

Hand-wringing clothing is ineffective and tiring. Crank-powered wringers are much more effective and wrung-out clothing will dry much faster indoors or out. Crank wringers are often sold by "country store" and "survival" suppliers for $80 to $120.

Drying Devices

Clothesline poles were a regular fixture in backyards until the early 1970s. There would be two poles approximately 6.5-feet tall with a

Crank-powered wringers are much more effective than hand-wringing clothes. iStock/ hipproductions.

cross bar at the top (like a telephone pole) and two to four spaced hooks for the clotheslines. These poles had to be strong steel or 4 x 4 wood and set deep into the ground or in cement to handle the pull of the wet clothing. The poles were usually about twenty to thirty feet apart, and the lines would be stretched taut between them. Clothing was secured by means of clothespins. Too much or too wet clothing could cause the cloths to droop to the ground so you had to use some judgment. There are still a number of folding clothes-drying racks on the market today. These are designed for indoor use but could be used outdoors if there is no wind.

Soap

Today we don't even think much about the importance of soap. It comes in thousands of forms and brands. We have special soaps for personal hygiene, dishes, household cleaning, and laundry. Not long ago soap was soap. It was all-purpose and not to be wasted. Bar soap was used first for bathing and then maybe laundry or dishwashing. When the bar got small it was placed in a device consisting of a screen ball on a wooden handle. You placed the soap remnant into the ball and used the handle to stir the soap into warm water. Voila! You have soapy water for laundry or dishes. Today we use way too much soap for most applications and throw away 20 to 40 percent of bar soap. In future hard times, soap will become a valuable commodity for personal use and for trade and barter. While soap can be made at home, it may take a while to do and the material may be difficult to come by. Soap must be a stock-up priority. A hundred bars of cheap soap would be an excellent investment now.

Making Soap from Scratch

Soap making has become a hobby. You can even get kits. There are lots of soap-making recipes and methods in self-reliance books and on the Internet.

The instructions that follow are for one bar, but you could bulk it up a bit. You will need 1/2 cup of cold water, two teaspoons of lye, and one cup of beef tallow. Slowly add the lye into the water. Then warm the tallow and the lye-water solution separately to about 100°F. Finally, mix the tallow into the solution with a whisk or similar mixer. You should get a thick yogurt-like product. Pour this into a bar-size mold and set aside to harden. After twenty-four to forty-eight hours you should be able to remove the soap from the mold. It will need to age uncovered in air for two to four weeks to fully solidify and cure.

Of course, the resulting product can be used for personal hygiene and other cleansing applications as well as for laundry.

Note: Commercial lye would be best for this formula, and the water in all cases must be soft. See page 96 for instructions for making homemade lye.

SOURCES

You can get purpose-made hand washer plungers, washboards, clothes-drying racks, and even a soap-making kit from Lehman's at lehmans.com.

CONCLUSION

Having the necessary skills and equipment to clean clothing with less electricity or no electricity will certainly be an advantage in the future. Returning to natural drying (indoors or outdoors) alone can result in considerable savings. This is one of the easiest and most practical self-reliance initiatives to achieve.

14

Clothing Repair and Production

The need for clothing is generally overlooked in survival scenarios. The supply of clothing throughout the twentieth century has been taken for granted. Marketing tricks and cheap foreign-made products have made clothing a disposable item for many. Sure, there are secondhand clothing drives and occasional drives to provide replacement clothing for disaster victims, but never a need to reconsider how to produce or replace clothing when the existing importation and distribution systems fail. Although our overstocked closets would probably outlast our food stocks, we would eventually need to repair and then produce clothing. Unfortunately, few homes have the skills and supplies necessary for this need.

A BRIEF HISTORY OF CLOTHING PRODUCTION

The first clothing was made from hides of animals, but the manufacture of cloth from wool, cotton, and silk dates back thousands of years. We will not go into hide tanning or cloth manufacture here. Before the industrial age, most people had a limited amount of clothing. Buying a new shirt, dress, or pair of pants was a fairly big expense for the average person. Buying a suit or topcoat was an event. Production of fabric and then the garment was the result of many hours of skilled work by hand. Sunday clothes were carefully protected, and work clothes were patched until they were completely worn out. Worn-out clothing was used as patching or rags or even towels. Cloth was valuable at any stage. A worn knitted garment might be unraveled and the yarn reused.

Many rural homes still spun yarn on a spinning wheel and produced cloth on looms. Almost every woman knew how to sew, and every older woman knew how to knit.[5] My grandmother was an expert at both sewing and knitting and produced most of my childhood mittens, sweaters, and scarves. The earliest home appliance was the treadle-powered Singer sewing machine. These early, nonelectric machines made it possible for a wife to provide virtually all the family's clothing needs for the cost of cloth and thread. Schools in Chicago still taught basic sewing machine and hand sewing into the late 1960s.

After World War II, both husbands and wives were pulled into the job market, where they would make taxable wage. This also meant that both spouses had to buy manufactured clothing, much of it imported from other countries. The home sewing machines were relegated to occasional use or just wound up in the alley (nonproductive video games and exercise machines have since replaced the productive treadle-powered sewing machine). Today, the great majority of people have no skills or equipment for clothing repair or creation. All of the newer home sewing machines are computer controlled and electricity dependent. You can still find treadle-powered Singers in antique shops and on eBay for $100 to $300. People with these machines and the skills and supplies (e.g., thread, cloth) to use them will do well in the barter-and-trade future.

---

5   Sewing was not considered "man's work" in the past. That need not be the case today or tomorrow.

Obviously, there is not enough room in this chapter to actually teach the skills of sewing, weaving, and knitting. Fortunately, hobby sewing and knitting are alive and well. Many communities have clubs with members who do these things. The Internet has all kinds of instructional videos and sources of equipment. Best of all, you probably have time to acquire the skills and supplies you would need.

If you prefer to start with a basic electric sewing machine, there are lots of good choices. All come with detailed instructions, and many are highly automatic. You could probably run one from a small generator or solar/battery system, but eventually you should try to get a treadle-powered machine, even if you don't use it right away. You will need to stock up on spare parts and any repair manuals you can get your hands on. You will also need bolts of cloth, such as denim, cotton, wool, and light canvas, as well as a wide variety of thread colors and strengths. And don't forget needles and lots of buttons.

Underwear and socks are the first garments that are going to wear out, and they are the hardest to make or repair at home. For this reason, I recommend stocking up on these items now. A hundred pairs of socks and a hundred pairs of underwear could be high value items for use or trade in the future.

Dyeing

While dyes can be made from natural sources, it would be a good idea to stock up on various colors of clothing dye for dyeing both your homemade clothing and salvaged clothing as may be required.

Natural dyes can be produced from alder bark (orange), onion skins (orange), carrot roots (orange), oak bark (tan), sumac leaves (tan), dandelion roots (brown), dandelion blooms (yellow), walnut husks (deep brown), boiled acorns (khaki green), coffee grounds (brown/black), and many other staining plants. To produce the dye, chop the plant material into small pieces and bring to a boil in about two parts water to one part plant material. Then simmer for at least one hour. Strain out the plant material. Before you dye the fabric, soak the clothes in fixing solution and wring it out. Fix the color for berry-based dyes by soaking the cloth in 1/2 cup of salt to eight cups of cold water. To fix plant dyes, soak in a solution of one part vinegar to four parts cold water. Place the fabric in the dye bath and simmer until desired color is obtained. Remember that the colors will look darker when they are wet than when they dry. Muslin, silk, cotton, and wool dye well with natural dyes but should be laundered in cold water thereafter. You will need a big pot for dying, and it will get stained.

Knitting

Knitting takes considerable practice and patience but very little equipment, and it can be done virtually anywhere you can carry two long needles and some yarn. It can produce caps, socks, gloves, sweaters, and other cool-weather garments. If you are going to add this skill to your capabilities, you will want to stock up on good-quality yarn. Knitting is a multistep process that is best learned from a teacher, but it can be learned (with patience) from books and videos.

Hand Sewing

Regardless of machines, you do need to know how to hand-sew. You will need to repair existing clothing as it gets damaged, and sew on patches or create a few basic garments by hand. So here are the basic steps for hand sewing.

Select a needle that is big enough to push through the fabric, but not big enough to leave a visible hole. Tougher fabric requires a bigger needle and tougher thread. Run a length of thread through the needle so that half of the length is on each side of the hole. Be sure you have enough thread (double) to complete the job. Tie a knot on the two loose ends of the thread. Start by pushing the needle through the fabric from the backside just before the start of the seam, not too close to the edge that it can tear through. Pull the thread through until it is stopped by the knot. Now put the needle through the

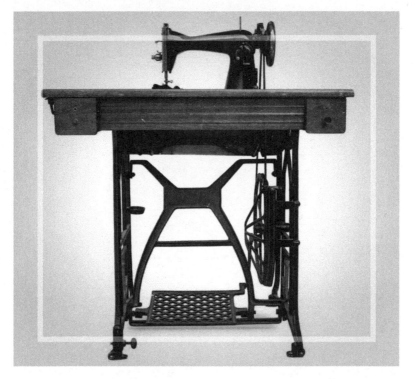

Classic treadle-powered sewing machines can still be found in antique shops and on eBay. iStock/Nakteve.

adjoining or overlapping fabric from the back. Continue repeating until the entire seam is closed or joined. Use small stitches for stronger seams. Finish with a very small knot, very close to the fabric.

The process is easier to do than to describe, and there are many variations in stitching. When sewing two pieces of fabric together, put them together with the backside facing out so that the stitches will show less. When sewing up holes, pinch the fabric together toward the inside and sew those edges to make a neater patch. A little practice is the only way to get it right. Remember, even cavemen did it.

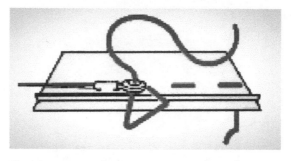

Simple over and under stitches from 1/8 to 1/4 inch apart.

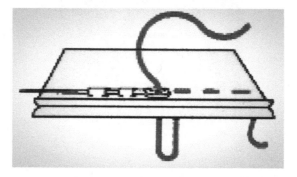

Stronger double stitch. Each stitch goes half-way back to overlap the previous one.

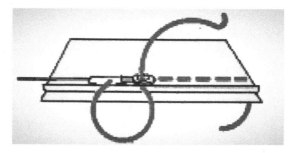

Patch stitched with seams folded inward toward the inside of the garment to look neater.

Weaving

Weaving is time consuming and thread consuming, but it can create cloth when supplies run out. Of course, this assumes that you have a big supply of thread or the ability to manufacture thread from raw materials, such as wool or cotton. There are many articles on how to build and use a hand loom. A loom can be built from available wood and hardware without special tools or parts. Loom operation is a bit too complicated to cover here, but it can be mastered by anyone and could be a great hobby that would produce clothing material and trade goods in the future.

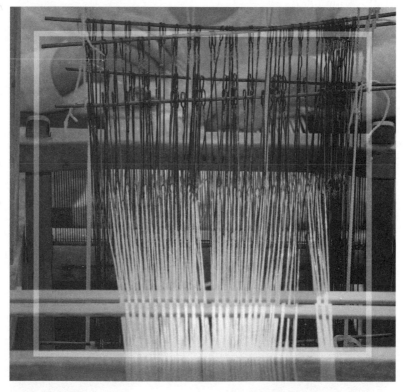

Home looms can be purchased or built at home. Folding and table tops looms cost $800–$1,000. This can be a great hobby and business, but depends on a sustained supply of yarn. iStock/ lukasok.

CONCLUSION

Although clothing may not be an immediate need, garments will eventually wear out and need to be replaced in a situation where replacement items may not be available. Stocking up on basic clothing would be a good investment for future needs and for trade and barter. Acquiring the basic skills and supplies for clothing repair should be considered part of anyone's long-term preparedness capabilities. Acquiring a sewing machine and building up supplies of cloth, thread, buttons, and spare parts will be essential for families and can provide alternative income and significant savings in the future economy.

Those who master the skills of knitting and weaving will have developed a rewarding pastime and a high-value self-reliance skill. Basic sewing can be mastered fairly quickly and should be learned by all in the very near future. Advanced sewing, knitting, weaving, and dyeing require more time and investment, but should be goals that are not put off.

15
Lights

A catastrophic failure of the power grid could plunge the entire country into chaos for years. Millions of lives and billions in property would be lost without power and light for even a few months. Even the inevitable increases in the cost of electricity as cheap fossil fuel is depleted will result in a drastic change in lifestyles and living standards. Increasingly frequent manmade and natural catastrophes bring darkness to urban and suburban areas. While so-called alternative power sources may stave off a complete collapse of the power grid, we must face the necessity of having emergency and backup lighting sources. We probably will not go back to the "dark ages," but we may well need to adjust to the coming "dim ages."

A BRIEF HISTORY OF LIGHT

Once early man had fire, he could function a bit after dark. The light and warmth provided a sense of security and was probably the first unifying technology that created tribes and communities. Universal and practical lighting is a fairly new development. Whale oil lamps, candles, and torches were pretty much the only light sources available until the later nineteenth century. Even these were expensive for the average person. Massive candlelit halls and well-lighted offices were reserved for the wealthy. The working class and the farmers had a dawn-till-dusk life.

Developed countries started using eliminating gas for urban buildings and streets toward the middle 1800s, but outlying areas remained dark. I actually remember the last gas lamp in Chicago (1945) being shut down, and I owned a building that still had working (though disabled) gas fixtures. Underdeveloped countries did not have electric lights well into the twentieth century. An escapee from the old Soviet Union told me that people in his village would travel miles to see the lighting at Communist Party headquarters. No, not electric lights—gas mantel lanterns. The introduction of electrical lighting in the late 1900s changed society more than anything in the previous two thousand years. Urbanization, three-shift industries, twenty-four-hour society, and all the modern medical, industrial, societal, and technological changes are founded on cheap and available lighting. When the lights go out, everything stops. If the lights stay out for more than a few days, chaos starts to develop.

SCENARIOS FOR DARKNESS

Short-Term Outages from Storms or System Failures

Almost everyone has experienced power outages ranging from a few hours to a few days. These are inevitable and will be more frequent and lengthier as environmental and economic conditions worsen. Electrical outages disable air conditioning, heating, communications, and other modern systems, but lighting is the most essential. Generators are great for short-term maintenance of sump pumps, water pumps, refrigerators, fans, and other necessities but are an inefficient way to maintain light alone.

Modern solar rechargeable and crank-powered lanterns, candles, and camping lanterns can provide adequate lighting for days or weeks. Today's LED flashlights and lanterns can provide sustained light for work and security. It is best to have a full variety of lighting options: rechargeable batteries, a solar battery charger, kerosene lamps, gas lamps, LP lanterns, and candles. Probably the Cadillac of lamps is the Aladdin kerosene mantel lamp. These lamps look great and provide good room light. You can get plenty of spare mantels and also a conversion kit to use wicks. They cost from $130 to $175. You should also have spare mantels and wicks for your lanterns. Glow sheets are great for providing "night-light" where you only need to see enough to avoid bumping into things.

Left to right: LP gas lantern, kerosene lantern, candle lamp with spare candles, LED electric lantern, and LED crank-/battery-powered lantern. Center: large light rechargeable glow sheet.

A variety of flashlights will be a good investment in the future. Top: older Maglite, heavy and weapon capable, but it is not very efficient. Left to right: solar chargeable 6-LED flashlight, headlight, high-powered "tactical" flashlight with variable power, and strobe.

Long-Term Outages

Short of massive nuclear war, there are few "man-made" disasters that could take down the entire national power grid for weeks or months. System redundancies and reserve capacities can restore most regional outages in a few weeks at most. A cyberattack on our electrical grid and generators has the potential of disabling the entire infrastructure (e.g., lights, computers, sanitation, water supply, transportation) for many months or even years. Electromagnetic pulse (EMP) weapons are generally of limited range, but a large-scale EMP generated by the sun could do considerable damage with consequences similar to a massive cyber attack. In some cases even alternative devices could be disabled. Small-scale solar and wind-generating systems now available in most home improvement stores would be a huge benefit. They should be supplemented with stockpiled candles, kerosene, and LP gas cylinders. Even bicycle-powered generators can be used to recharge batteries. Nevertheless, air conditioning, big-screen TVs, and other luxuries will have to be abandoned in favor of light, heat, and maybe a fan. At least limited power should be restored within a year or two regardless of the cause of the disaster.

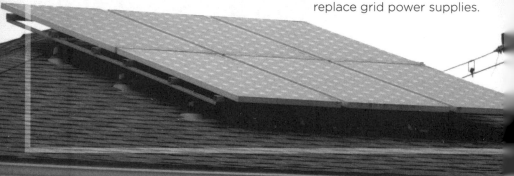

Typical solar panel array on roof. Solar power options can range from portable panel units for charging batteries and running small appliances for a few hundred dollars to large roof-mounted systems that back up or replace grid power supplies.

Small wind turbines like this cost only a few hundred dollars and can be used to run pumps or charge batteries when solar power is low. iStock/tillsonburg.

HIGHER AND HIGHER COSTS

While solar, wind, and some improved nuclear power sources may sustain the supply as cheap fossil fuels run out, it is highly unlikely that the current supply can be maintained or the existing low costs continued. Certainly the cost of lighting and other electric-dependent utilities will rise to the point where it will force most people to use them sparingly. No more decorative or landscaping lights. No more wasted lights in unused areas or rooms. Even streetlights and area lighting will be limited. In some places rolling blackouts and rationing will be enforced. It is difficult to predict exactly how severely this cost/supply issue will impact our lives in the coming decades, but it will happen. Having alternatives and self-reliant options to bridge the gaps and lower the costs will put the survivor ahead financially and provide a higher level of comfort and safety.

CONCLUSION

The era of massive and cheap illumination is ending, but effective and reasonable alternatives should provide all necessary and effective lighting for those who prepare. Occasional and localized blackouts should be no more than an inconvenience to the well-prepared citizen. Long-term blackouts are less probable but not impossible. Such an event would disable all vital life-sustaining services and bring total chaos for an extended period. Preparing for this kind of catastrophe and providing light would be just one of many challenges for the survivor. Nevertheless, a restoration of lighting would be essential to immediate survival and eventual recovery.

16

Tools for Self-Reliance

The ability to make and use tools effectively pretty much defines civilization. The society with the best tools wins. Remember the first scene from the movie *2001: A Space Odyssey?* There is not much we can do without tools.

Tools may be simple, hand-held items or huge, powered devices, but they mostly do one of two things: they cut or they pound. Such tools as saws, files, screwdrivers, and wrenches are found in just about every home. Most of them are fairly durable and many can last a lifetime if properly used and maintained. I have a few tools that are at least fifty years old and function like new. Having maintained a one-hundred-year-old historic landmark building, I have lots of plumbing, electrical, and heavy maintenance tools. Most homes have at least some basic tools for minor repairs and assembling those "some assembly required" items. The change from repairable to disposable furniture, appliances, and structural materials, combined with a trend toward powered and cordless tools and the introduction of cheaper imported tools, creates a potentially serious tool shortage in the future.

A BRIEF HISTORY OF TOOLS

The first tools were made from stones, wood, and bone. As metallurgy improved, they were made from bronze, iron, and steel. Most of the basic hand-tool designs have been around for more than three thousand years. The tools used during the American Civil War were much like the ones the Roman army would have used. Only the advent of the steam engine and then the electric motor changed the nature and capacity of tools. We could cut, pound, and crush on a much greater scale.

Before the late nineteenth century, the average person had a very limited number of tools: a few shovels, hoes, saws, hammers, axes, and maybe a file or two. Most repairs were made by nailing, so screwdrivers and wrenches were not in the home tool chest yet. Of course, craftsmen would have many more specific tools depending on their needs. Carpenters would have a lot more drills, saws, chisels, planes, clamps, and wood files. Blacksmiths would have all kinds of special hammers, tongs, punches, and files. The industrial revolution put millions of repairable machines into the home and supplied the homeowner with a plethora of tools to repair those products.

The automobile necessitated a variety of wrenches, pliers, screwdrivers, and other devices that were previously not needed. The emergence of hobbies also fueled the home tool industry. As a child I had real, small-sized tools in my Handy Andy toolbox, including saws, files, awls, and drills. Yes, things that could hurt someone, but every kid knew how to use tools and to be careful. Working with tools was taught in all schools and was a respected skill.

Before World War II, most home workshops consisted of hand tools alone. A few home shops had a few table saws, drill presses, and even machine lathes, but they were the exception. Right after the war, there was a big push to sell power tools to the masses. This came together with a housing boom and a big increase in auto sales. New homeowners started building porches, lawn furniture, and other improvements. The autos of that time tended to need constant service, much of which could be done by the "home mechanic." The home shops of the mid- to late twentieth century tended to be pretty well equipped, but more and more energy dependent. Corded power tools and then cordless versions replaced hand tools. Various pneumatic tools replaced even automotive wrenches. There is very little work that cannot be done by a portable powered device today. Additionally, manufacturers started producing unrepairable or disposable products. The two-job/two-income family made it more practical to buy new than to fix things or to pay others to do repairs. Today the average home has fewer hand tools, and more of the tools are power dependent. Very few have any kind of hand drill, and most drive screws with a powered screwdriver. Driving a nail straight or making an accurate handsaw cut is a rare skill.

As the supplies of cheap products and energy become scarce, the need for repairing and, in some cases, rebuilding older equipment will increase dramatically. Manufacturing spare parts and even entire devices from available materials will be a necessity.

WOODWORKING TOOLS

Fortunately, there are a lot of good manual woodworking tools still on the market. You will want to stock up on wood files, sandpaper, and drill bits. Purchase good saws that can be repeatedly sharpened. The same goes for chisels and planes. You will need to have a drill sharpener, grinding wheel, and fine metal files for sharpening tools. I explored many hardware outlets, and not one had a hand-powered drill. Some younger employees had no idea what I was talking about—drills have motors! I found both bit brace and hand drills still available online at www.baileighindustrial.com, or you may find them at hardware stores near Amish communities. The bit brace cost $104, and the hand drills ran from $30 to $50. You will also need a variety of the large-diameter bits for the brace, which are harder to find. Maybe you will get lucky at a yard sale or flea market.

Bit brace and hand drill; the only alternative when the power goes off. Wikipedia/Jayess.

You will also need a variety of clamps and a supply of glue. Glue doesn't keep indefinitely so you may need to make your own. Below is one formula for glue. There are many others you should know.

How to Make Milk Glue

1. Place 1 cup of milk into a glass jar.
2. Pour 1 tablespoon of vinegar into the jar.
3. Stir slowly.
4. Allow mixture to stand and separate.
5. Slowly pour the separated mixture into a colander.
6. The solids will remain in the colander.
7. Scrape up this substance with a putty knife and place on a paper towel.
8. Squeeze as much liquid as you can from the solids through the paper towel; repeat.
9. Place the remaining substance into a second clean jar.
10. Add 1/8 cup of baking soda and work into the mixture. Add a bit more if it is runny.
11. You now have good wood glue.

METALWORKING TOOLS

The most important function of metalworking tools is the ability to repair and make other tools. In the past people never threw away metal. Iron, steel, brass, copper, and other metals could always be cut, bent, heated, melted, cast, and reshaped. When a pioneer cabin was abandoned, they would burn it down to recover the nails, hinges, and other metal used in its construction. Nails, bolts, nuts, screws, wire, and banding will be very difficult to manufacture, and you should stock up on them. Hacksaw blades, emery cloth, metal files, and metal drilling bits should also be stockpiled. Metal stock—such as bar stock, tubing, and sheet metal of various gauges and types—would be a good investment. Metalwork involves a lot of bending, pounding, and cutting, so you need a variety of hammers, a good heavy vise with an anvil back, or a separate anvil.

ALTERNATIVE POWER

Almost anything can be made with hand tools, but the time and effort required to precisely cut, drill, mill, or turn metal or accurately cut quantities of wood can be prohibitive. Waterwheels or animals on treadmills powered sawmills and trip hammers long before steam or electricity. Treadle-powered lathes, drills, grinding wheels, and other machines produced good-quality items hundreds of years ago and are still common in third world shops. I once held a copy of the British Webley revolver that had been made from stolen railroad rail steel and machined on treadle-powered equipment in the backcountry of Pakistan by the rebels. Converting any of the existing "powered" equipment to generators, solar, or manual power would be well worth the effort. Even bicycle-powered generators running a table saw or lathe would beat doing this work by hand.

Treadle Power

A treadle is simply a device for converting the up-and-down (rocking) motion of your legs and feet on the flat treadle to a turning motion of a wheel. Belts can be used to adjust the speed and power of the device (e.g., sewing machine, lathe, grinding wheel, drill), and flywheels can store energy.

RESOURCES

Now is the time to stock up on various repair manuals and how-to books. It is unwise to become dependent on the Internet for information, making manuals and books more valuable than ever. In this case older and used books are probably better than newer ones that assume the use of power tools and other modern equipment. With the noted exception, most of the tools and supplies recommended are still available at hardware stores. A full line of woodworking tools can be found in the Lee Valley catalog (leevalley.com). Lehman's (lehmans.com) carries some tools and other Amish equipment. Coleman's Military Surplus (colemans.com) often has good surplus tools at reasonable prices.

CONCLUSION

The end of the disposable society and the decline in availability of many items will make the ability to repair and maintain household equipment, furniture, and appliances a necessity. The ability to manufacture or rehabilitate equipment will provide potential income and tradable skills. The acquisition of carpentry, metalworking, and repair skills and equipment should be a priority now. Developing these as hobbies today will certainly turn them into valuable self-reliance skills in the future.

17

Transportation

"In traveling by [rail] road, I thought that the perfection of rapid transit had been reached. We traveled at eighteen miles an hour at full speed. This seemed like annihilating space."

This is how Ulysses S. Grant—then a citizen, later the commanding general of the Union Army during the Civil War, and eventually the eighteenth president of the United States (1869–1877)—described his first train ride in 1839.

Up until the early 1800s, humans traveled at the walking speed of three to five miles per hour. A horse could get you up to fifteen to thirty miles per hour for a short while, but the average speed was about the same as a walking man. Animals could move more people and cargo but not much faster. Sailing ships took weeks to cross the Atlantic and over ninety days from New York to San Francisco.

The age of coal and steam brought steamboats and locomotives that revolutionized transportation. Coal and steam still dominated into the mid-twentieth century. I can still remember the ground shaking as huge smoke- and fire-spouting locomotives roared past my Chicago neighborhood. After World War II, internal combustion and jet engines revolutionized ground and air travel once again, but have been consuming nonreplenishable fuels at an escalating rate.

While desperate attempts to find more natural gas and petroleum and develop alternative sources of fuel continue, it is clear that the age of cheap transportation is drawing to a close. In the 1960s we dreamed of going to the stars; now we talk of electric cars, bicycles, and windmills.

REALITY CHECK

While the government and the media talk about "going green" and "alternative fuels," and hoped-for miracle breakthroughs, the reality is that we are running out of fuel and time, and have no practical replacement for the cheap, easy-to-transport fossil fuels that created the miracles of the twentieth century. The economy as we know it, the world as we know it, and the population as we know it cannot exist without the unlimited fuel that we no longer have. What is sustainable and attainable will never match the speeds and tonnages of current transportation systems. Consider the following:

- People are not going to commute thirty to fifty miles to work each day on a bike, especially in winter!
- Electric cars may get us around town or downtown, but electric semitrailer trucks?
- As usage of the airports, expressways, and interstates declines, who is going to pay for their maintenance?
- Do we see electric- or solar-powered container ship or airliners? Really?
- Batteries, hydrogen production, wind power systems, fuel cells, and solar power systems are all dependent on petroleum products and rare earth materials that are already nearing depletion.

World trade and travel as we know it will grow increasingly expensive as alternative energy buys time to adapt. Localization of manufacturing will replace globalization. Long-haul trucking, container shipping, interstate expressways, and air travel will decline. State and county governments will reassert economic and political power. The whole way we live will need to change. Farms, homes, schools, factories, and trade centers will have to be brought closer together. High-speed electric rails will have to replace most long-distance automotive and air transportation. Foreign involvement and wars will become less practical since ships, tanks, and planes take a lot of fuel, which won't be readily available.

Large cargo ships will be less practical as fuel sources grow more expensive. Wind power or even coal/steam power may come back in some form, but world trade as we know it will change.

TRANSPORTATION ALTERNATIVES IN THE LATE TWENTY-FIRST CENTURY

Automobiles and Trucks

Internal-combustion-powered vehicles will be around for several decades. It is difficult to predict the way in which hybrid, alternative fuel, and electric vehicles will evolve. The issues of how they age and recycle have not been addressed. Ranges and efficiency are going to improve but will never reach the unlimited power and range of petroleum fuels. There will probably be methods for converting internal-combustion engines to run on alcohol and other "renewable" and homemade fuels. The problem there is that you will probably have to carry all your fuel for a round trip with you, since there may not be any alcohol or wood-gas fuel stations on your route. So your range may not be better than an electric car. It looks like the age of cruising the open roads at high speed in your big Cadillac or (more likely) Chevy truck will soon be over. A very sad situation!

Bicycles

There is a big push to get people to ride bicycles. The newer ones are lighter and easier to ride than the old ones of the 1950s and 1960s. Riding is healthy and provides a method of escape when roads are closed. Mile for mile, a bike is more efficient than walking and permits you to carry more survival gear. You can comfortably cruise at about ten miles per hour, about three times faster than walking. Most communities have plenty of dedicated (no cars) bike trails that would also provide escape routes if needed.

My bicycle with its survival trailer. Note the water bottle and rear cargo rack. A mountain bike is recommended for its ruggedness and stability on rough ground.

The current problem is that bikes are somewhat hazardous when mixed with automotive traffic. No practical and safe way has been found to put bikes next to automobiles and trucks in city traffic or on the sidewalk with pedestrians. As motor transportation declines, this problem may be less acute, but bikes have a lot of limitations.

The elderly and those with certain physical issues can't use them. Rain, snow, cold, or extreme heat makes riding them miserable and dangerous. They offer no protection against collisions or criminals. Even with a trailer, your carrying capacity is limited. Now we all know that the streets of third world nations swarm with bicycles of all descriptions carrying people and goods, and we can learn and adapt these methods, but remember that they are third world countries.

Horses

Horses may come back in rural and even fringe suburban areas where they can still be fed and kept. Back in the 1950s there were still some horse-drawn rag wagons in Chicago. Horses are the ultimate ATV, but they require lots of care and food. I love to ride them, but others just never get the hang of it. I recommend that everyone try riding if they can and do it regularly if they like it. It's a great and healthy sport and could be a good escape method in an emergency.

Public and Commercial Transportation

Ugh! I hate taking public transportation, but it will be a big part of how we get around. Unfortunately, it will still get more expensive. Certainly rail and bus service will grow as auto and air transportation declines. Private enterprise will probably provide some practical and affordable alternatives for short- and medium-distance travel.

We won't be going back to steam locomotives or horse and buggy, but new kinds of railroads will take the place of trucking, automobiles, and air travel in many applications.

Boats

Powerboats consume a lot of fuel, but sailboats might be practical for river and Great Lakes travel. Even wood- and coal-fueled steamboats could make a comeback depending on circumstances. It is something to consider if you live near waterways or the coast.

Walking

For the first forty years of my working life, I walked to work, a distance of four miles. Earlier in my life when I was a student, I walked to school: grammar school (four miles), high school (three miles), and college (three to four miles). To this day, I never drive anywhere if it's less than two miles away.

The health benefits of walking are well established. Good news: if you make walking a regular part of your routine, you're going to get healthy and lose some weight. In the gravest disaster, you may have no alternative but to walk to safety or just walk everywhere. Refugees carrying bundles, pulling wagons, or pushing carts have fled and survived time and time again. While we can hope that it never comes to that, you should be able to hike and carry a pack for some distance. Walk as much as possible. Take up backpacking. This healthy habit could save your life.

CONCLUSION

How long our sources of fossil fuel will last and how much we can do with alternatives is difficult to predict, but drastic changes are inevitable by the middle of this century. As our society and economy become less mobile, our communities, lifestyles, and options will change drastically. The mobility that has facilitated trade, freedom, wealth, and centralization will give way to a slower and more localized world. Imaginative and adaptive means for retaining freedom of movement must be pursued, but adaptation of traditional methods (bikes, walking, etc.) should be established early. A balanced approach of reducing the need to move while retaining the ability to move freely should be followed.

18
Trade and Barter

This chapter deals with economics in a post-collapse world. Why a collapse? The entire economic system is a myth. True value is based on the existence of needed and usable products, services, and raw materials balanced with the need/demand for them. America has spent far beyond what it actually has in natural resources and productivity. We do not have the materials or production capacity to pay or work our way out of debt. Once the world realizes that the dollar is worthless, a collapse must follow. At best the collapse will be a crumbling process as crisis after crisis forces government, corporations, and individuals to downsize and economize. There will be less and less, which will cost more and more.

- The depletion of fuel (petroleum and natural gas) and other natural resources will continually raise prices for everything. While prices will go up, people will have fewer jobs and less money to pay for these goods. Luxury items, newer vehicles, entertainment, new homes, travel, and higher education will be deferred for food, shelter, and clothing. Government welfare programs and special interest programs will be cut, resulting in considerable disturbances and protestations.

- The climate change will dramatically increase the cost of food while reducing the supplies. Climate-driven disasters will continue to cost billions that we can no longer afford. Recovery will not happen or will be done at the expense of other critical needs.

- Perhaps, most important, the economic distribution is totally unstable. Ideally, the large middle class would hold about 50 percent of the nation's wealth (e.g., property, stocks) with about 25 percent going to a lesser number of poor and rich. We all know that never happens. The common belief is that the middle class and poor together may hold 30 percent of the national wealth with the rich holding about 70 percent.

The reality is that the large number of poor, middle class, and semi-rich hold less than 10 percent of the nation's wealth while a few ultra-rich individuals hold more than 90 percent. This imbalance is a result of decades of government and federal bank manipulation and policies. Such a disparity is bound to result in violent economic disruption and possibly revolution. This is why the ultra-rich are pouring billions into antigun and anti-preparedness political campaigns. Money is the ultimate power. One billionaire overrides hundreds of millions of voters. There is no democracy, equal representation, or equality in such an unequal economy. Something has to—and will—give.

A BRIEF HISTORY OF ECONOMICS

The earliest forms of "economics" were simply examples of tribal interdependence. Everyone in the tribe did his or her "fair share" and shared the results of foraging and hunting. As specialties evolved, some degree of trading was necessary. For example, a skilled arrow maker was entitled to some of the food gained by his devices. More complex trade-and-barter systems developed as farming and crafts evolved. Produce and products were brought to the "marketplace" on "market day." But what you could have was still limited to local production and craftsmen.

More ambitious traders, moving by land and sea, distributed local products farther afield for wealthier individuals who could afford the prices. Intermediate trade goods—such as gold, silver, and salt—facilitated more complex exchanges of goods and services. But basic trade and barter still dominated well into the eighteenth century. The age of coal- and petroleum-driven trucks, ships, and planes made nationwide and international trade dominant in the twentieth century.

Paper currency and now computer data has replaced virtually all forms of item-for-item and service-for-service trade. Unfortunately this "IOU-based" system freed from any standard has led to massive imbalances and inequities. All efforts to correct these developments have only led to further problems. Ultimately, the value of currency and treasuries is completely out of line with the available goods, services, and materials. The current world economy exists on credit that is based on myth.

WHAT WILL HAPPEN?

Looking at the economic realities, it seems likely that the economy will bounce up and down for decades, with the downs always exceeding the ups and the disparity between the super-rich and the dwindling middle class always growing until we fall or slide into disaster. The three phases below will happen over a long period but will overlap. It may be argued that they are already in progress.

Phase One (Disaster)

The existing economy will collapse suddenly or in stages. As this happens, unprepared people will exhibit panic and desperation. Prepared people and groups will fall back on their supplies to survive and to trade for existing supplies. The unprepared may be willing to trade gold, silver, and jewelry for essential goods, but few will want these useless items. Communities may develop marketplaces and trade rules early on to prevent conflicts and looting.

Phase Two (Survival)

As it becomes apparent that "recovery" is going to be a long process, more organized trading systems will evolve. Formal marketplaces, market associations, trading agents, co-ops, and mobile traders will develop. A black market, raiding gangs, and protection groups will also emerge to skim from every trade. Here again is the need for strong protection provided by the traders themselves. At this stage there will be no intermediate currency (e.g., gold, silver): only goods for goods, service for service, and service for goods. Those who can provide essential services (e.g., medical care, mechanical repairs, transportation, and carpentry) or produce essential goods (e.g., food, clothing, and medications) can survive in this economy. Of course, there will be a strong need for skilled and unskilled labor, so anyone willing to work should be able to secure shelter and food in exchange. Those who possess land, shelter (e.g., buildings), tools, and raw materials (e.g., wood, metal, chemicals) will have the foundation to employ others to produce food and products or to trade land, tools, or shelter use for other goods and services.

Phase Three (Recovery)

The new economy will be more local and regional, but traders and trade associations will facilitate the exchange of goods and materials from region to region. Long-distance trade and a "global economy" will be far less feasible in a fuel-depleted world. What "currency" will be used to negotiate trade is hard to predict. Paper IOUs based on actual goods will only have value if they are enforceable by established rules and actual consequences for not paying. Gold and silver may again have value as nonessential goods become available. The

Internet may well survive and provide the platform for a noncurrency, trading economy. Electric rail transport and alternative energy vehicles will move goods but not near as economically or extensively as the cheap petroleum vehicles of the twentieth century.

WHAT TO DO?

Money can still be made in stocks and gold for a while, but you cannot risk your whole savings there. Any gains made in these markets should be used to acquire marketable skills and hard goods. Short-term survival preparedness must come first. Dips in employment, periodic recessions, and other challenges may stall your preparations and deplete your stores. Temporary spikes in the economy may encourage procrastination, apathy, or even risk taking. Stay on track to self-reliance!

- Stock up on hard, tradable goods like socks, nonperishable foods, ammunition, nails, seeds, and soap.
- Invest in real estate and land. This is a constant, usable commodity. Don't get caught up in the investment value. Consider it a resource to provide shelter, workspace, crop-growing land, and water collection.
- Learn a practical trade, such as machine work, carpentry, sewing, or health care.
- Practice trading at swap meets, flea markets, and eBay.
- Start your own business, but be sure it's one that will still be in demand once the economy gets tight.
- If you are in a big family or a preparedness group, you can establish a program for trading goods and buying wholesale to save everyone money. In this way you will already be semi-independent when cash loses value and goods are unavailable.

THEN AND NOW!

We recovered from the Great Depression because America had an enormous untapped reserve of oil and natural resources and a great number of skilled workers who could produce real (not virtual) value. Four years after the Japanese bombed Pearl Harbor on December 7, 1941, America had crushed Germany and Japan while simultaneously supplying millions of trucks, tanks, ships, and planes to both the Western allies and the Soviet Union. The damage done at Pearl Harbor amounted to just two-day ship production in 1943. Today our reserves are mostly used up and our industrial production capacity is a fraction of what it was. We have been living on the credit built up by our past resources and labor for decades. Now it's gone.

On September 11, 2001, a handful of terrorists destroyed two buildings in New York City, damaged the Pentagon, and crashed four planes. Fourteen years later we are still fighting in a Stone Age country and our economy is dying. What should this tell you about our true situation?

19

Fire Suppression and Survival

Without the intervention of fire departments, many cities and parts of most suburbs will burn during a prolonged survival disaster.

INTRODUCTION

Disasters often result in broken power lines, ruptured gas pipes, and spilled flammables. At the same time, fire departments are over-loaded, undermanned, and may be unable to even get to the fire scene. Longer-term emergencies usually involve the use of lanterns, candles, stoves, and heaters, which greatly increases the potential for fires. As the economy declines, the manpower and equipment available to fire departments will be reduced. The capacity to prevent, put out, or escape fires becomes increasingly important in a family survival and self-reliance program.

HISTORY OF FIRE AS A DESTROYER

Long before there were nuclear weapons, fire was the primary destroyer of towns and cities. Firebombs killed far more people and did far more destruction in World War II than explosive bombs and nuclear bombs combined. The 1945 Operation Meetinghouse fire-bombing raid on Tokyo killed more than 100,000 people, burned approximately fifteen square miles of one of the world's most densely populated cities to the ground, and left about a million people home-less. The glow from the firestorm could be seen 150 miles away. The German city of Dresden was virtually wiped out with 100,000 dead from a firebombing a month before the Tokyo raid. By comparison, the atomic bomb dropped on Hiroshima killed 35,000 people. His-torically, accidental and arson fires have devastated Rome (AD 27), London (1666), Chicago (1871), and Boston (1872).

Fortunately, modern building codes and greatly improved fire-extinguishing equipment have prevented the spread of urban and suburban fires in the past century. The danger of massive fires is only held at bay by our relatively flame-free environment and the quick responses of fire departments. In a general collapse situation, mul-tiple uncontrolled fires would be inevitable for the following reasons:

- In a general collapse situation, people will be using candles, heaters, and flammable fuels more often. Many of them will not be trained or vigilant enough to prevent fires from starting.
- Broken gas pipes, leaking fuel tanks, and downed power lines will create intense fires that cannot be extinguished at the source.
- Looters and arsonists will be uninhibited by law enforcement and will start fires in commercial and residential areas.

- Once started, a fire doubles in size about every sixty seconds. Without prompt response from a fire department, any fire will totally involve the structure within five to ten minutes of ignition.
- Structures within several hundred feet of a burning building will ignite from the heat, and burning embers may ignite buildings hundreds of yards downwind.
- If there are a sufficient number of adjoining structures burning, they may generate a firestorm that will move like a tornado through a built-up area until it encounters an open (no fuel) area or consumes all of the fuel.

If you live in an apartment building or closely spaced housing development, your only hope is to establish control and ensure vigilance of the whole building or block. If the house next door or the one next to that goes up, you are doomed. A fire in the next block or across the street may or may not spread to your home. Being able to put out burning embers will be crucial. Again, you have to protect every home on your side of the street. This will require organizing your neighbors early.

In the unlikely event that you still have water pressure, you can use garden hoses to dampen roofs and walls and to put out embers. A garden hose is useless once a structure has caught fire. Unless you have a functioning fire pumper truck and several hoses from an unlimited water source, you are not going to put out a house fire. There are affordable systems that can supply fifty-plus gallons per minute (GPM) at high pressure through a 1.5-inch hose. These systems could prevent fire from spreading to adjoining structures, but at fifty-plus GPM, you would need 1,500 gallons of water for thirty minutes of firefighting. You might consider having an inflatable pool or water tank that could be filled in anticipation of such an emergency.

FIRE PREVENTION

Of course, the one thing you can prevent is your being the source of a fire. With no fire department and limited water supplies, even a small fire in your home can consume your whole home and then your whole community. In most cases, your home is still your best survival shelter. You will be using candles, oil lanterns, gasoline generators, and other fire hazard devices. Keep these in safe locations, well away from paper, clothing, fuels, and other combustibles. Fill gas tanks and lanterns outside well away from structures. Store flammable fuels outside. Be aware of carbon monoxide hazards. Have both smoke and carbon monoxide detectors in working order. Have at least two full, large-fire ABC fire extinguishers and have one on hand whenever handling fuels. Don't wait for the fire to start before reading the instructions! Your local fire department may offer training in extinguisher use.

INCIPIENT FIRE EXTINGUISHING

Unless you have a fully functional fire pump and hose system, you cannot hope to put out a structural fire. But if you have immediate and effective fire extinguishers, you can put out "incipient" fires started by candles, cooking equipment, heaters, and even a Molotov cocktail. You can also put out trash fires, brush fires, and windblown embers from other structures. Good dry chemical extinguishers rated for ABC class fires are available in many sizes. Class A fires are paper, wood, and cardboards. Class B fires are burning liquids such as gasoline, grease, and kerosene. Class C fire is electrical. Your ABC extinguishers are good for all three, but any kind of water spray can be used to extinguish a class A fire.

The most important thing about a fire extinguisher is its location. They must be right there at hand when the fire starts. A few seconds or a minute spent getting the extinguisher can mean that the fire is beyond control by the time you get back. So you must have one in the kitchen, garage, furnace room, shop, and anywhere else that you have an open flame (e.g., fireplace, stove, candles) or flammable fuels.

Using Fire Extinguishers

When using a pressurized powder extinguisher, you should stand well back from the fire and aim just short of the front edge of the fire to let the powder roll over the flames. Then sweep back and forth, going just past each side and farther in with each sweep until past the back of the fire. Don't squirt; keep sweeping. Be sure all flames are out before stopping. Then hold ready for re-ignition. Don't blast the fire close up! This will only blow burning fuel around. Be careful not to walk into the fuel as you advance on the fire. It is always best to have a second person at your back with another extinguisher ready. Never let the fire get between you and your escape route. Never try to fight a fire once the room is filled with smoke.

When fighting a class A fire, soak the fire thoroughly and then use a shovel or other device to turn over the fuel and soak hot spots. Consider that a fire goes up and out and looks for fuel and air. It may follow vents, electrical openings, and other routes to ignite in between walls or in other rooms. Search and destroy it and stay alert for rekindling for up to twenty-four hours.

EVACUATION FROM A FIRE-RAVAGED AREA

There are many photographs of refugees fleeing through the fire and smoke of burning cities in Europe during World War II. What a horrible fate! Your survival packs, caches, and plans should serve you well if fleeing becomes necessary. Your route and speed will be unlike evacuating from a pandemic or other situation. You will need to act quickly once you determine that you are in the path of the fire. Your priority is not so much distance as direction. Take a route that will get you out of the fire's downwind and uphill path, and out of the fuel supply of closely spaced buildings and woods. Seek open, grass-free fields and empty places. During the Great Chicago Fire, many people fled out into Lake Michigan.

PROTECTION OF VALUABLES

Unless you are sure that fire is not likely in your area, you should take some precautions.

- Consider relocating out of high-density areas or apartment complexes.
- Move valuables and important documents to a fire-safe location. During World War II, civilians often buried valuables in their backyards so they could recover them after the fires burned out.

Typical fire extinguishers available at most home supply stores. Bigger is better. Inspect extinguisher regularly. The larger ones on the right can be refilled and repressurized.

- Move children, pets, and the elderly out of the fire area ahead of time. Your only hope may be to run to escape the fire, and they can't.
- Always be ready to evacuate with everything you need to survive. Fire spreads very fast. You will not have time to find, gather, and load what you need once it comes your way.

FIRE SURVIVAL

Since fires may start and spread through populated areas at any time, it will be necessary to post a twenty-four-hour watch. This will also guard against looters and arsonists. If you awaken to a smoke-filled room, do not sit up! The air just above you may be heated to several hundred degrees and filled with toxic gases. Roll out of bed and crawl to the nearest exit. You have only seconds. A dust mask and a flashlight kept in the bedside drawer may save your life in the dark smoke-filled house. Once outside,

Garden sprayers are good for class A fires. As a last resort, a very fine spray might retard a class B fire. iStock/mlhalec.

never return to a burning building. You will not come out again! You should have trained every member of your family in fire-escape techniques and have designated a meeting place outside. To illustrate the need for training and speed, I offer the photos on the following pages that I took at a test fire recently. This was set up as a normal-size living room where a fire started in the sofa.

CONCLUSION

Fire is often an overlooked side effect of other disaster scenarios. Storms, earthquakes, epidemics, economic collapses, and other events could create ideal conditions for the spread of massive fires through urban and suburban areas. Fire can negate all your survival planning and preparations. Fire prevention, escape, and survival must be part of your survival planning and equipment priorities.

Fifteen to twenty seconds after ignition: smoke detectors go off. If you spot this fire immediately and have a good fire extinguisher, you might be able to put it out; if not, you have only about sixty seconds to get everyone out.

Sixty to ninety seconds: heavy smoke and gases obscure visibility down to a few feet above the floor. You must stay low and get out immediately.

Two to three minutes: the heat of the fire begins to ignite other materials. The TV explodes and hot, combustible gases fill the room.

Three to five minutes: a "flashover" of the hot gases explodes the fire throughout the structure.

Five minutes: fire department arrives on scene. Even this fire hose would not be enough to extinguish a totally involved structure. The best it can do is to prevent the flames from spreading to adjoining structures.

20
Home Defense

For most people, armed combat will be one of the worst experiences of their lives. There is nothing enjoyable or gratifying about it. If it can't be avoided, hope that you are mentally and physically equipped to survive it.

It is impossible to foresee exactly what kinds of home-defense situations will develop from a slow degeneration or a sudden collapse of civil order. The situation that any individual or family finds itself in will vary from an increased danger that never develops into actual confrontations to one that could even escalate into military level combat. Those living in or near large urban areas will certainly face different challenges than those in small towns and rural areas. Therefore, the planning, training, and armament required to survive in and move through these areas will be different. Moreover, the requirements for initial short-term survival combat will differ greatly from those of long-term sustained security.

A BRIEF HISTORY OF LAW AND ORDER

In primitive societies, after diseases, murder is the most common cause of death. In the absence of organized and effective "police" (by whatever name), the strong and the violent will always steal, rape, intimidate, and kill the weaker population. It is this very fact that causes and justifies collective security. Ancient and medieval societies did define "crime" and enforce laws, but only for the benefit of the landed class and only within close geographic boundaries. The common folk and those living in the outer lands had to depend on the family and the clan for protection and revenge. This is still the case in the third world and in many urban communities today.

In the absence of modern record keeping, communications, and forensics, the identity or even the existence of a criminal or a victim was difficult to establish. Unless someone was caught in the act, the individual almost always got away with it. Criminals simply moved to new grounds. Even at the beginning of the twentieth century, many folks who left the farms for the big city simply disappeared without a trace.

Modern police force detectives only evolved in the late nineteenth and early twentieth centuries. Even today, "law and order" depends on the values and attitudes of the communities. While most crimes are committed by a very small number of career criminals and gang members, a much larger percentage of people would engage in criminal behavior (e.g., assault, rape, looting, burglary) if there were no expectation of arrest or consequences. In the absence of law enforcement, criminals and gangs would have no deterrent to attacking the general population unless people are armed and prepared.

REALITY CHECK

The authority of the state is a myth, only maintained as long as it is respected and accepted by the majority of the people. Once this myth is cracked, law and order evaporate. If a massive disaster overwhelms the existing police and military, or they are rendered ineffective by massive popular unrest or inadequate funding, chaos will soon develop. Once the general population loses respect and confidence in the authorities, there is no authority. Even the most brutal dictatorships cannot survive a general loss of confidence or fear. The whole Union of Soviet Socialist Republics collapsed in spite of the KGB and the military. The so-called Arab Spring brought down several strong governments in Northern Africa and the Middle East. Mexico is ruled by the drug cartels, not the state.

Once this process starts, the police will focus on protecting their families and the governments. Government agencies at all levels will concentrate on defending their families and associates. Citizens will be left on their own gradually or suddenly. Theft and looting will start with established criminals, but as conditions worsen, desperation will lead to foraging and violence by normally law-abiding citizens. We will look at three scenarios that could develop in the next few decades.

Scenario 1

A gradual decline in the economy, energy supplies, and funding for the police results in increasing street crime and occasional outbreaks of looting and rioting. There is an increase in home invasions and gang activities. Gangs begin to loot food stores and trucks and now operate a black market for essential goods. Police respond slowly and generally back off in the face of large numbers.

Self-Defense Situations and Preparations

In the early stages of this scenario, you may still be going to your job or legally gathering supplies, but now you need to be much more alert and well-armed. Any restriction on carried armament should be ignored in favor of survival. If possible, travel in twos or threes. Avoid urban commercial areas where looting, crime, and gang activities will be heaviest. Look poor and don't get followed home!

Good high-capacity handguns with extra magazines will be a must for the streets. Even short-barreled shotguns or carbines may be appropriate. If you have been wise enough to have a supply of food and water on hand, and maybe a network of support, you will not need to "forage" or go to the black market for your needs. If you are not prepared and networked, you will be forced to risk combat every time you run out of canned goods or toilet paper. Ambush is always a possibility.

Of course, the fact that you are not venturing out may attract attention, so you will need to be ready to detect, discourage, and eliminate any would-be invaders. In this scenario, attacks are most likely to be by individuals or small untrained gangs. They will probably just try to kick in the door or rush through when you come in or go out. They may also try to take a family member hostage outside and then force you to let them in. For this reason, anyone going out should be armed, covered, or accompanied by an armed family member even near the house. When you are inside, all doors should be closed, locked, and blocked. Even at home everyone should carry handguns, and defensive rifles and carbines should be loaded and handy. At night, lights should be out and window exposure should be avoided. Spend time in the basement and interior rooms if possible. If a twenty-four-hour watch schedule is not practical, sleep with your weapon nearby. The hours between dusk and dawn are the most dangerous. If order is not restored, the situation may degenerate into scenario two or three within a few weeks.

Scenario 2

A sudden and total collapse of the system caused by a natural disaster, epidemic, or financial collapse plunges the society into chaos. Stores and malls are being looted and burned. Gangs roam the streets and invade homes with impunity. Police, medical, and fire services are nonexistent. Millions flee urban areas as food supplies, water, and sanitation systems fail.

Self-Defense Situations and Preparations

If you live too near to major highways or commercial districts where mobs and looters will kill and destroy everything in their paths, you will be forced to flee by vehicle or on foot to safer areas. Other books have covered movement through high-threat areas, and evacuation gear and camps. Suburban communities and homes may still be defensible and even sustainable for the well prepared and well-armed. Smaller towns and rural homesteads will need to be prepared to fend off occasional roaming groups of motorized or walking assailants. Using outposts or good binoculars to spot and identify approaching threats on roads and trails will be essential. You will need medium-range, high-volume carbines for built-up environments where large numbers of "enemies" may get fairly close before being spotted.

You will need a reliable semiautomatic carbine with at least one thirty-round magazine and plenty of extra magazines to stop or drive off close threats. If you live in more open terrain, a long-barreled semiautomatic combat rifle or bolt-action, scoped hunting rifle will be needed. Your options will be to fire a warning shot at range to redirect intruders past your location or pick off well-defined threats before they get to you. Remember, you can't just shoot every person who comes down the road, and even your warning shot may initiate a battle that did not need to happen. That person may be innocent or even a potential friend. A single person or small group may also be a scout for a larger group coming behind. Think carefully before starting an engagement under these conditions. And consider that if you have had to evacuate, *you* may be the target for someone out there with a scoped .30-06 and no hesitations about shooting. This is a great reason to be able to stay home.

In this scenario your rifle is your primary weapon and your handgun is your backup weapon. At this stage, block or community patrols may be needed. A good "Crime Watch" program may be a good foundation for this and could even be supported by the existing police establishment under such desperate conditions. Roadblocks may be necessary to sort out and reroute refugees and potential raiders. It would be far better and more humane to provide some food and water to refugees and route them around the town than to just block them.

Let's hope things don't get this bad, but remember that they have in other places at other times. Once order is gone, anything can and will happen.

Scenario 3

After a general collapse, centralized government is not able to restore constitutional liberties and security. An unconstitutional and oppressive state attempts to restore order based on force and oppression, or smaller more localized gangs or extremists attempt to establish regional dictatorships by force. General resistance and military-style combat break out in many areas. Most people are forced to choose sides, but even neutrals are likely to be attacked in some areas.

Self-Defense Situations and Preparations

This is the situation that most survival novels envision: a simple "kill or be killed—everyone who is not with you is against you" situation. It's not going to be that simple. You are going to have all kinds of combatants and noncombatants, disguised enemies, friends, and terrorists all mixed up on the field. Veterans from Iraq and Afghanistan can relate to this kind of asymmetrical war. Out of the initial chaos there will emerge dominant gangs of criminals and a variety of militia-like forces. Some of these will be *Mad Max*-like roaming bands while others will establish territories to dominate. It is impossible to predict what sort of alliances will form or what remnants of government may reemerge. The economy and the society will be badly fractured, and a lot of evil people will try to manipulate and prey on a lot of desperate people.

Control of food, water, and other resources will be the key to power. If criminal gangs or would-be dictators are able to provide safety to their supporters and offer the only sources of food, water, and other critical needs to the population, they will win, even if they are brutal and oppressive. If a significant force of good and benevolent people is strong enough to provide and defend these resources, then recovery with liberty will be possible. It will take a heroic and determined population to hold back the forces of hate, prejudice, and greed that will certainly emerge. In this long-term situation, only organized and trained citizens will be able to restore order. This will mean defending one's own family and community while respecting those of others. It will be essential to be strong enough to deter and defeat any threat while being ready to unite to rebuild the society.

Obviously, here you need to have very good military-style weapons and lots of ammunition. You also may want to consider having extra weapons for currently reluctant neighbors, relatives, and friends who will be willing to help once things get more threatening. Good binoculars, night vision equipment, camouflage clothing, smoke bombs, and other types of equipment would be helpful. If you do not have military training, at least get some good manuals on small-unit tactics and get lots of shooting practice with each weapon. Do not forget spare parts and maintenance items for each weapon.

If the situation degenerates to this point, our country and the world will truly be in the dark ages for a long time. It may never recover. The greater the force of responsibly armed and well-prepared citizens, the less destruction and disruption there will be.

CONCLUSIONS

Survival combat will be a complex combination of home defense, street combat, and military tactics unlike anything previously experienced. In some cases it will be necessary to take or hold ground, but more often sheer survival will be the priority. While casualties will surely be incurred, the concept of acceptable losses can hardly be justified when those losses are your children, parents, spouses, and close friends. Casualties cannot build the future.

Only well-armed, well-prepared, and well-organized people will have the option of survival. They will be able to deter, fight, or retreat as needed. If you are preparing for survival without preparing to defend your life through all anticipated situations, you may be stocking supplies for someone else. Starting with a good handgun for self-protection, you need to build a small battery of weapons appropriate for the kinds of situations that may develop five, ten, or twenty years from now. These items and the ammunition for them will become increasingly unavailable either because of government regulation or popular demand as the crisis grows more obvious. While your family, budget, location, and health may all play a part in your capacity for various types of combat, there is no excuse for surrendering through inaction, procrastination, or complacency.

RECOMMENDED WEAPONS

For Home and Street Defense against Criminals and Backup

The debate goes on between the advocates of 9mm and 40- and 45-caliber handguns. The thing to know is that a handgun is an inherently inaccurate weapon. Even the police score only 10 to 20 percent hits in real combat. These weapons are to stop immediate threats in the ten- to fifty-foot range and drive away identified threats out to a few hundred feet. You will want to have a high-capacity automatic with extra magazines. Revolvers are great bedside drawer and under-the-car-seat guns because of their reliability, but they are a bit bulky and slow to reload.

Glock autopistols have a well-deserved reputation for reliability and durability under rough conditions. Made for combat, they have no safety. They come in a wide variety of sizes and calibers from 9mm through 45 caliber, and magazine capacities ranging from ten to seventeen rounds. If you prefer a more conventional weapon with visible hammers and safeties, Colt, Browning, Beretta, Heckler & Koch, and SIG all make fine choices.

Glock large-frame autopistol: reliable firepower with high-capacity magazines.

For Home and Street Defense under Civil Disorder Conditions

The AK-47 is the most successful military rifle in history. These rifles fire 7.62x39mm ammunition. These weapons are comparatively cheap and come in a variety of configurations. The folding-stock models are good for interior and street combat. The reason AK-47s are preferred by unconventional forces is that they can be abused and poorly maintained and still be reliable. There are lots of magazines and accessories on the market, including one-hundred-round drum magazines. Gun stores and gunsmiths will not be around in some situations. The AK is not as accurate or light as the M16 and its clones, but it costs much less.

The M16 and its various clones and copies are fairly durable and reliable weapons. The problems with earlier versions have been corrected. Ammunition and parts are commonly available. There are lots of add-ons, such as lasers, flashlights, night sights, and even a device to simulate full-automatic fire. You can get a carbine version for close defense or long-barreled variants for combat in open areas. These cost from $900 to more than $2,500 depending on manufacturer and design.

Military-surplus AK-47 with folding stock sells for about $500.

Shotguns such as the Mossberg 500 and Remington 780 12-gauge pumps are great for heavy-duty home protection and street combat. The wide range of ammunition includes slugs, buckshot, breeching (for knocking down doors), nonlethal rubber, flamethrower, and armor piercing. Shotgun shells are easy to reload if you stock up on powder and primer and a few tools.

For Home and Street Defense under Full Combat Conditions

The AK-47, AKM, M16, and a variety of other so-called "assault rifles" will suit your needs here, but stocking up on magazines and ammunition would be well advised. Night vision attachments would also be a good investment. If you can afford to add a long-range, high-accuracy rifle, do so.

The Mosin-Nagant 7.67 bolt-action rifle is a cheap but reliable weapon for those on a very strict budget. It is a very old design but fairly accurate. The Russians dumped hundreds of thousands on the market after refurbishing them. They are priced from about $100 to $200. During World War II both the Finns and Russians used them as sniper rifles to very good effect.

A better, but more expensive, choice would be the Remington 700, which is the civilian version of the M40 sniper rifle used by the military, or maybe a Steyr SSG 69.

One of the many commercial versions of the US military M16.

21
Education

The educational system in America is leading the way to collapse. The existing system was developed for an urban, industrialized society that no longer exists. Various experiments have extended the existence of these big centralized systems but have not corrected the fundamental flaws that guarantee its collapse. Declining enrollment, obsolete methods, and bankrupt states and municipalities are rapidly bringing education as we know it to an end. These "schools" have been failing in their fundamental duties for decades, while disparaging patriotism, self-reliance, and individual responsibility. The sooner these systems are replaced by high-quality, local, and family education that is independent of federal and state funding and interference, the better it will be for future generations.

A BRIEF HISTORY OF EDUCATION

Up until the mid-nineteenth century, education was reserved for males of the elite and wealthy class. Some basic "Three-Rs" education was available in country schools, followed by apprenticeships in the trades. Those who did attend these country schools were held to a high standard. My father only graduated from sixth grade but had impeccable spelling and handwriting, and could do the complex math required to be a stationary engineer. I once read a fifth-grade test from a pioneer school of the 1800s—I doubt if many postgraduate students of today's colleges could have passed it.

The industrial revolution brought the need for workers who could read, write, and calculate. So, the modern urban school system was born. Children were regimented into classes (departments), from which they were promoted or demoted. They responded to the bell (whistle), and came out nice, obedient employees. The late twentieth century ushered in computers and the idea that everyone needed a college degree. In order to do this, colleges initiated government loans and lowered the standards significantly. The result is a lot of people who owe a lot of money for useless degrees. Of course, the banks and the schools made a lot of money. That's what it's all about.

My educational experience started in 1947 just after World War II. The population was exploding, and new schools were being built every year. There was no busing in the city at that time, so I walked several miles, winter and summer, to the grammar school I attended the last two years. There were no gang territories to be concerned about then. By the time I got through the eighth grade, my school was using trailers as schoolrooms. During my high school years, things got pretty rough. In the 1960s things started changing in the South Side of Chicago. I was working two part-time jobs and living in one room. I walked two miles to the school, two miles back, and then three miles to my jobs and back every day. I had no time for homework and I was often tired, but I made it. There were standards that had to be met regardless of the situation. I took classes in business, engineering, and chemistry in junior college until they were completely taken over by the gangs. Later, I obtained a number of certifications, but my most valuable knowledge came from a bit of homeschooling, lots of reading, and personal experience.

My observations since then have been that current graduates of city colleges are significantly less educated than I am. In addition, they have been misled and brainwashed regarding history, economics, and values. It appears that standards are low and curriculums are not well rounded. Today's youth are not dumber, but they are treated as if they are. While there are certainly brilliant minds and valuable citizens coming out of the schools today, they are far outnumbered by undereducated, miseducated, and misinformed victims of the broken educational system.

The focuses of education should be on building a firm foundation of reading, math, and writing skills combined with values and responsibilities. High standards and reasonable, consistent discipline must be restored while recognizing the individual qualities and challenges of each student. We must provide and insist on the basics, improve the weaknesses, and recognize and support each student's gifts and strengths. Every effort must be made to help and improve the troubled and difficult student, but never at the expense of the sincere and striving students.

As I stated, my father only made it through sixth grade in a rural southern school, but his penmanship was perfect and his mathematics were sufficient to pass an engineering examination. My twelve years at city schools in the 1950s fell short of his six years in the 1910s.

LIBRARIES

Paper books are rapidly being replaced by online publications. The modern generation has grown accustomed to accessing all information on a computer or mobile device. This is great, really, but there are all kinds of scenarios where these systems will fail or one has no access to them. Also, these sources are monitored, tracked, and even modified by others. In the gravest extreme, access to the very information you need most could easily be denied. In such a world, paper books become even more valuable.

Print out and save information found on the Web. Buy and safely store every book on self-reliance, medicine, crafts, mechanics, chemistry, and similar subjects that you can find. Build up a library of old schoolbooks for all grade levels. Ninety-nine percent of what worked in a 1912 schoolbook will work today for teaching reading, writing, and arithmetic.

INTERNET SCHOOLING

Internet education is available today and may survive some future collapse scenarios. If "the grid" survives, online education will be a major element in the future of education. These courses can run from $600 per semester for grade school to more than $3,000 for higher education. Considering that you have already been taxed for the existing, poor-quality system, this may not be practical. If you do go this route, be sure that you are using a certified and recognized school whose credits will be accepted by colleges.

FAMILY, GROUP, AND COMMUNITY SCHOOLING

The so-called "home schooling" movement has been around for decades and has developed a great system of materials, standards, and curriculums. These can be supplemented with parentally selected materials to provide a much better primary and secondary education than public schools do. However, this approach requires a full-time home teacher.

Education clubs and larger families can more easily share the costs and time required. Small communities or preparedness groups can use the homeschooling materials and other resources to organize local education groups. Currently, there are plenty of homeschooling courses and materials available on the Internet. There is also a lot of information about the laws and regulations regarding this educational option. As the existing system breaks down, many regulations will need to be changed or will just become irrelevant, but for now you should be sure that your education program will meet local and state curriculum standards and ensure that students will be able to pass any required tests. Any large preparedness group with a significant number of children would be well advised to research the potential for establishing a group school.

APPRENTICESHIPS

It is a good bet that in a post-collapse world, the apprenticeship (training for service systems for learning technical and trade skills) will return. A contract is made whereby one promises to perform basic work for a period of time at low wages in return for training. The teacher gets cheap labor, and the student gets free training. A win-win. At the end, no one is in debt, and both have profited. Preparedness groups with skilled members should consider applications of this method now.

CONCLUSIONS

Although the twentieth century expanded educational opportunities, it made compromises for political and social reasons that lowered standards. The late efforts to expand college through grants and programs resulted in the mass distribution of worthless degrees to debt-ridden students. The declining populations in urban areas doomed the school systems. Urban public school systems and "traditional" centralized education in general are failing and collapsing. The future belongs to private, personal, practical, family, and local educational systems. The education survivor would be well advised to establish educational goals based on what the practical needs of a collapsed/rebuilt society will be. A combination of Internet learning, self-training, and local education clubs and schools will be a practical, effective, and affordable replacement for the costly and ineffective systems that are now crumbling.

22
Energy

The entire existence of the universe, time, and our civilization is dependent on energy. Biology is simply a system for acquiring stored energy, releasing it, and using it to gather more energy. Energy is life; the loss of energy is death. The wealth, power, and survival of a nation and civilization are directly related to its access to energy. The essence of survival is fuel, shelter, food, water, and warmth. In other words, Energy = Survival.

A BRIEF HISTORY OF ENERGY

The citizens of ancient Rome and the soldiers of the American Revolution would not have had too many differences between them. Other than gunpowder, the technologies and methods of combat were much the same for more than two thousand years. Energy sources were wood-burning systems, animal power, human muscle, and a bit of wind and water. Chemistry, medicine, agriculture, and metallurgy had changed very little. That same soldier would be completely unable to comprehend the society that exists now, just over two hundred years later. Why?

The industrial age started in the very late 1700s with coal. This fossil fuel supported the development of steam-powered railroads, shipping, electrical power generation, water pumping, large building heating, and sewage systems into the mid-twentieth century. Petroleum and natural gas enabled mass transportation, urban sprawl, flight, medicines, fertilizers, insecticides, chemicals, and a population explosion. It also enabled global wars, more centralized governments, and the so-called global economy. These fuels eventually replaced coal in most applications. As the populations increased, the use of these limited sources of energy increased exponentially. The entire "life as we know it" system became totally dependent on an energy source that is exhaustible and irreplaceable.

AS THE FUEL RUNS OUT

The most optimistic estimates give us fifty to eighty years before oil and natural gas are gone. *Gone!* Solar, wind, hydrogen, and even nuclear energy technology is dependent on petroleum technology. No miraculous (e.g., cold fusion) replacement for oil and natural gas has been, or is likely to be, found. Do not fall for the phony "free energy" or "endless oil" junk science. Long before these sources are exhausted, they will become unaffordable until it takes more than a barrel of oil in energy to extract, process, and distribute a barrel of oil. The market and the government know this now. Conservation is not about the environment; it's about money and buying time.

Climate change is a fact regardless of the cause. More extreme weather is here and will exacerbate the problems of energy depletion. The cost of heating the overpopulated far northern cities and cooling the overpopulated far southern cities will be unsustainable. The costs associated with disaster response, rebuilding, and flood control will ruin economies and fail.

This is not an apocalypse—it is a slow disaster. We have time to adjust, and the market is already trying to find alternatives. The problem is that the existing economy, society, and population cannot survive these adjustments.

Even without the effects of climate change, food production will drop dramatically. The massive farm machinery, fertilizers, and pesticides that made industrial farming possible will be gone. Producing massive amounts of food on huge farms and transporting it in refrigerated trucks or airplanes will be completely unaffordable. Food shortages will impact the third world first (it already is) but will ultimately cause unrest, revolutions, and even outright wars throughout the world. Land will become the new source of wealth, and food will be the new oil as it was in the past. We may well see the return of the big landowners and sharecroppers. The big urban centers are too isolated from the food sources to do well, even with urban gardens. Suburbs and smaller towns having more land per capita, and those closer to farm areas, should be able to develop support systems. The bottom line here is that we will not be able to feed this population, and we will not be able to sustain the supermarket, prepackaged, fast-food culture we have today.

There will probably be more limited and expensive electrical power, but massive lighting of cities and affordable air conditioning are unlikely to survive. Home heating will become a major problem as gas and oil become scarce. Most homes today were never designed to be heated by electricity or coal, even if conversion were possible. Wood-burning stoves are nice, but there will not be a tree or a fence standing within two to three years near any urban area if wood is the primary fuel source. A lot of people are going to freeze. We could return to coal-fired steam for municipal water pumping, electrical generation, and sewage pumping, but the populations of urban areas have trebled since this was used and the infrastructure and systems no longer exist. Those of us who remember coal and steam know that it is inefficient and smoky. Back in the 1950s industry, railroads, and homes still used coal. In the winter the snow turned black within a few days. Steam also heated skyscrapers, but newer buildings were not constructed to be retrofitted, and the systems (usually tunnels) that brought coal in and ashes out are long gone. I know this because my father was a stationary engineer in a forty-story building and he spent lots of time around high-pressure boilers and huge steam-powered pumps and generators.

Cheap, portable fuel has created a commuter society where our jobs, schools, homes, and supply sources are all widely separated. Before the 1960s, most folks could walk to the stores, and many could walk or take public transportation to their jobs. There were no expressways, malls, bedroom communities, or massive parking lots. Families had more time at home, knew their neighbors, spent less on food and fuel, and needed only one job per family to pay all their bills and save money in a local bank. They paid fewer taxes and needed far less government intervention. They also generated less waste and did more for themselves.

It is unlikely that electric cars will be able to sustain the same mobile society and even more unlikely that we will see solar-powered semitrailer trucks, passenger planes, or container ships from China in the late twenty-first century. Limited vehicles on slower roads and more public transportation will give the advantage back to small and local economies and governments. There will still be manufacturing and government, but they will be very different. These transitions will be at best distressing and at worst violent and traumatic. While world wars and big government may be less likely, national and local conflicts and the attempts by fanatics and demigods to take advantage of the people will increase. Only large-scale public self-reliance led by responsible organizations can prevent their success.

Society will not return to the eighteenth century, but it will not directly progress as it has for the past 150 years. With an energy-depleted world we will have to do more with less, and there will be fewer of us. There may yet be some scientific breakthroughs to at least partially replace the cheap, free energy that brought the miraculous advances of the twentieth century, but that is a long shot. Almost all the breakthroughs were because of oil in the first place.

Homes will return to a more industrious state: gathering and storing water, growing and processing food, cooking more meals, doing more maintenance and repairs, generating more of their own energy and heat. That will probably require at least one person who works at home and children to pitch in. Here again, larger families and networks will have great advantages over isolationists and loners. It will take very aware and determined people and families to make the dramatic adjustments and sacrifices necessary to survive and thrive in the new reality. Those who stay in denial will suffer greatly. Those who adjust will at least survive . . . some will even thrive and lead.

CONCLUSIONS AND ENTREATIES

The future does not have to be a retreat back to nineteenth-century life, nor does it need to be a brave new world of deprivation and authoritarianism. Yet there can be little doubt that life will be very different at the end of the twenty-first century and that the road from here to that future will be fraught with conflict, struggle, and disasters.

The world that most Americans have been brought up in has been one of gratification, security, comfort, and dependency. The concepts of individual responsibility and self-reliance have been forsaken for the easy and safe life where the necessities and even luxuries are consistently available and some agency or service is always there when things go wrong. We have had a very unusual and temporary period of cheap and unlimited energy, stable and serene climate, and consistent growth in population and economic wealth. Now we enter decades where strength, preparedness, self-reliance, and adaptability will be most needed. Americans must quickly adjust and retool physically, mentally, and morally. Those who continue to be in denial are planning to be victims. Be aware that many predators are waiting to take advantage of future events and trends. Determine now that you and your family will be survivors and will thrive.

The only hope of avoiding chaos and oppression is for self-reliance to become a core value and goal for a significant portion of the American population. We cannot hope to survive alone or in small insular groups for long. To own the future, we must advocate, educate, and organize while we can. Things will happen and things will change—that is unavoidable—but we can happen to things and we can determine how those changes affect our children and us. This book is only a starting point and offers some ideas.

While we cannot predict exactly what will happen, how it will happen, or when various changes and events will occur, we can predict with certainty that a succession of disasters and traumatic changes has started and will continue far into the next decades. You are urged to make plans and set goals to declare your independence and establish your survivability. We can come through these challenges as a stronger, safer, smarter, and freer people, but ultimately that is up to you.

I wish the reader, their families, their friends, and their communities the best success in their plans and efforts.

The beginning or the end—your choice.

PERSONAL DECLARATION OF INDEPENDENCE

Now it becomes necessary and prudent to reject the ties of dependency and vulnerability that have put at risk my life, liberty, and property, and to reassert the human right to have and exercise all means for personal survival, self-reliance, and self-protection. I hereby declare my intentions to achieve personal independence by:

Acquiring the skills, supplies, and equipment necessary to survive emergencies and disasters without outside help if necessary.

Being able and ready to help my friends, neighbors, and community in times of need and emergency.

Consistently increasing my capacity to provide the necessities of life to myself and my family independently of the society, state, and economy.

Opposing any restrictions or regulations or actions that would interfere with the right and ability to pursue personal preparedness and self-reliance.

Supporting all organizations and technologies that strengthen and expand the capacity of the individual to achieve and practice a prepared and self-reliant life.

I hereby pledge to the world my dedication to the cause of freedom and personal independence through preparedness and self-reliance.

Signed _____   Date _____

ABOUT THE AUTHOR

James C. Jones was born in Chicago, Illinois, in 1941. His early life situations required that he survive with little help at a very early age. Survival skills developed for the streets of the South Side of Chicago and in the nearby woods and marshes fostered a dedication to survival independence and self-reliance. The sports club he organized in high school evolved into Live Free USA, a national organization that has advocated for family preparedness and self-reliance for more than forty years.

Jones has written numerous articles for survival publications and appeared on various television shows promoting self-reliance. He is a certified emergency medical technician and hazard control manager, and holds certificates in training management from the Langevin Institute in Canada and in safety management from the American Society of Safety Engineers. He served as an award-winning safety and environmental manager for a Fortune 200 chemical manufacturer for two decades. He is currently retired and living in northwest Indiana, where he continues to write about and teach survival and preparedness.